Saint John Bosco
Champion for the Young

Written by Emily Beata Marsh, FSP
Illustrated by Wayne Alfano

Pauline
BOOKS & MEDIA
Boston

Library of Congress Cataloging-in-Publication Data

Marsh, Emily, author.

  Saint John Bosco : champion for the young / Written by Emily Beata Marsh, FSP ; Illustrated by Wayne Alfano.

  pages cm.—(Encounter the saints series ; 34)

  ISBN 978-0-8198-9045-0 (pbk.)—ISBN 0-8198-9045-6 (pbk.)

 1. Bosco, Giovanni, Saint, 1815–1888—Juvenile literature. 2. Christian saints—Italy—Biography—Juvenile literature. I. Alfano, Wayne, illustrator. II. Title.

  BX4700.B75M28 2015

  271'.79—dc23

  [B]

                                    2014046058

Cover art/Illustrated by Wayne Alfano

All rights reserved. No part of this book may be reproduced or transmitted in any form or by any means, electronic or mechanical, including photocopying, recording, or by any information storage and retrieval system, without permission in writing from the publisher.

"P" and PAULINE are registered trademarks of the Daughters of Saint Paul.

Copyright © 2015, Daughters of Saint Paul

Published by Pauline Books & Media, 50 Saint Pauls Avenue, Boston, MA 02130–3491

Printed in the U.S.A.

SJB KSEUSAHUDNHA11-131079 9045-6

www.pauline.org

Pauline Books & Media is the publishing house of the Daughters of Saint Paul, an international congregation of women religious serving the Church with the communications media.

2 3 4 5 6 7 8 9   21 20 19 18 17

To my parents, with gratitude and love

Encounter the Saints Series

Blesseds Jacinta and Francisco Marto
Shepherds of Fatima

Blessed James Alberione
Media Apostle

Blessed Pier Giorgio Frassati
Journey to the Summit

Journeys with Mary
Apparitions of Our Lady

Saint Anthony of Padua
Fire and Light

Saint Andre Bessette
Miracles in Montreal

Saint Bernadette Soubirous
And Our Lady of Lourdes

Saint Catherine Labouré
And Our Lady of the Miraculous Medal

Saint Clare of Assisi
A Light for the World

Saint Elizabeth Ann Seton
Daughter of America

Saint Faustina Kowalska
Messenger of Mercy

Saint Francis of Assisi
Gentle Revolutionary

Saint Gianna Beretta Molla
The Gift of Life

Saint Ignatius of Loyola
For the Greater Glory of God

Saint Joan of Arc
God's Soldier

Saint John Paul II
Be Not Afraid

Saint Kateri Tekakwitha
Courageous Faith

Saint Martin de Porres
Humble Healer

Saint Maximilian Kolbe
Mary's Knight

Saint Pio of Pietrelcina
Rich in Love

Saint Teresa of Avila
Joyful in the Lord

Saint Thérèse of Lisieux
The Way of Love

Saint Thomas Aquinas
Missionary of Truth

Saint Thomas More
Courage, Conscience, and the King

*For even more titles in the
Encounter the Saints series,
visit: www.pauline.org/EncountertheSaints*

Contents

1. The First Dream 1
2. Acrobat for God 7
3. Good News 13
4. Following God's Call 19
5. The Beautiful Lady 29
6. The Contest 36
7. A Good Friend 42
8. In the Seminary 48
9. Don Bosco 55
10. The Beginning 62
11. The "Flying Oratory" 71
12. Will He Live? 79
13. A Special Project 86
14. An Important Step 92
15. A New Student 98
16. Mama Margaret 104

17. The First Salesians 110

18. Grigio 117

19. Daughters of Mary, Help of Christians. . . . 126

20. "Love One Another" 132

Prayer. 139

Glossary. 140

1
THE FIRST DREAM

Nine-year-old John Bosco was in the middle of a fight. All around him boys were yelling, screaming, punching, and hitting.

"Stop it! Stop it!" John yelled as he ran around the field. But shouting at them wasn't working! *Maybe if I start hitting them, they'll stop hurting one another*, he thought. John kept darting between the fist-fighting, screaming boys. Suddenly he bumped into a kind-looking woman.

"Don't hit them, John," she said in a soft voice.

Startled, John looked around. *What is happening?* he thought. Now the boys had become wild beasts!

"Be gentle, John," the woman said. "You will win their friendship if you are gentle."

Instantly, the wild beasts turned into little lambs. Confused, John looked at the woman. She smiled.

"Lead these lambs to pasture, John. Take care of them. Later you will understand."

Then John woke up. He realized that it had all been a dream.

❖❖❖

Nine years earlier, on August 16, 1815, Francis Bosco called to his sons Anthony and Joseph. "Come, boys! Your new brother is here!"

Seven-year-old Anthony and two-year-old Joseph crept into the bedroom where their mother, Margaret, was propped up on the bed holding a new baby.

"Here he is, boys," Margaret whispered. "This is John."

Francis lifted Joseph up so he could touch John's hand with his finger. Anthony stood behind him. Francis looked at his family and smiled.

"Tomorrow we will take him to Saint Andrew the Apostle Parish in Castelnuovo (Kah-stel-NWO-voh) to be baptized," he said.

Francis took the newborn to the church while Margaret stayed home to recover from childbirth. The parish in Castelnuovo d'Asti (Kah-stel-NWO-voh DAH-stee) was the closest church to the Bosco's small village of Becchi (BEK-ee) in northern Italy. Only one day old, John Melchior Bosco was baptized there on August 17, 1815.

"This is a special boy, Francis," the priest remarked.

"Yes, Father," Francis replied. "All my boys are special: Anthony, Joseph, and now John. We are blessed, Father."

Francis Bosco was a farmer and a handyman. His first wife had died, leaving him with one son, Anthony. Francis married Margaret Occhiena (O-KYAY-nah), and their son Joseph was born in 1813, just two years before John.

Francis, Margaret, and their three boys lived with Francis' mother in a stone cottage on a small piece of land. They worked hard and lived simply. John's home was a happy one. Surrounded by love, the little boy grew quickly.

"Joseph," Francis called from the field, "run and tell your mama that we are almost ready for lunch. Anthony and I have been working hard all morning and we are hungry!"

"'Un-gwee!" little John mimicked, clapping his hands. He held up a worm to show his papa.

"Let that go, John," Francis laughed. He picked his son up and swung him to his shoulders. "Let's have lunch, boys."

"Here are my men!" Margaret smiled at her husband with their three sons in tow. "Come, come . . . lunch is almost ready."

Margaret handed Joseph the plates to put on the table. She took little John from Francis and scrubbed his hands. A few minutes later, the family was sitting down to their midday meal.

"Let's thank the Lord," Francis said. They bowed their heads as Francis led them in a prayer. The sun shone outside and a poor but happy family enjoyed their meal inside. Thankfulness and laughter filled their house . . . for now.

❖❖❖

During the week, the Bosco family worked hard on their small farm. Francis also worked for a man on one of the neighboring farms. Every Sunday, the family walked to Castelnuovo for Mass. One-year-old John liked to watch the priest and the altar servers. He knelt very still when the priest lifted up the Host and the chalice.

"That is Jesus, little John," Mama Margaret liked to tell him. "Jesus loves you!"

Walking home from church one day, Francis and Margaret watched their three boys run ahead of them.

"It's almost May, Francis," Margaret said. "Father will be having a Rosary procession at the church each night."

"Yes, just like he does every year," Francis replied. "Do you think all the boys are old enough to go?"

"Anthony and Joseph went last year," Margaret said. "But John is still just a baby. . . ."

"He is so attentive at Mass, though," Francis spoke slowly. "There's something special about the way he watches the priest."

"You're right," Margaret said. "We will bring him."

May came quickly, and the Bosco family joined in the nightly Rosary processions at the church.

One May evening, Margaret called to Joseph, "Go tell your papa to come in from the field. It's almost time to leave for church!"

Joseph obediently went out to the field. Francis was already walking toward the house.

"Why are you so late, Francis?" Margaret asked. "We have to leave."

"Margaret, I'm so tired tonight," Francis said. "It was very hot today, and I had to clean out the neighbor's cellar at the end of the day. It was so cold in there."

"Are you feeling ill? Maybe you should stay home?" Margaret asked as she buttoned John's coat. "There is some soup on the table. Eat some and go to bed. Rest will be good for you. You have been working very hard."

When Margaret and the boys returned home that evening, Francis was already in bed. But the next morning, he was still in bed. Three days later, he was very sick with pneumonia.

The next day, with Margaret, Anthony, Joseph, and John gathered around his bed, Francis died. John was not quite two years old.

Margaret led her sons out of the room. "No, no," little John protested. "If Papa doesn't come, I don't come."

Margaret knelt down by her youngest son. "Your father has gone away." She paused. "You don't have a papa here, little John."

This sad conversation remained John's earliest memory—his mother kneeling beside him, hugging him, and whispering through her tears, "You don't have a papa here, little John."

2

Acrobat for God

Mama Margaret paused in the doorway of the room where her three sons were sleeping. It was very early, but it was time to wake them up to begin their chores. Since Papa Francis' death, the Bosco family had worked very hard to keep up their farm. Anthony was now eleven years old, Joseph was six, and John was four.

"Boys," she said gently, "it's time to get up."

Anthony rolled over. Joseph squinted and stretched, and John propped himself up on one elbow.

"Good morning, Mama," he said.

"Good morning," Mama Margaret smiled. "Get dressed now, boys, and then we'll say a prayer to start the day."

After prayers each morning, the Bosco boys milked the cows, led them out to the field, fed the chickens, gathered wood, and brought in water. Then, after a simple breakfast, Joseph and John walked to school while Anthony helped Mama Margaret on the farm.

When Joseph and John came home, they scampered out to the field. There was always a lot to do on the Bosco farm!

"What are we doing today, Mama?" John asked.

"Hello, boys!" Mama Margaret was kneeling in the dirt. "How was school? Did you find the bread I left for you on the table? Joseph, please help Anthony with the hoeing, and Johnny, you can help me plant these seeds."

"Okay, Mama," John sat down next to his mother. Mama Margaret showed him how to plant the seeds carefully and quickly.

Each day, Johnny helped Mama Margaret with a different chore: planting, picking vegetables, shelling corn, stacking wood, baking bread. In the evenings after dinner, Joseph and John studied while Mama Margaret mended socks and shirts.

One such evening, Mama Margaret put away her mending.

"Come, boys," she said. "It's time to say a prayer before we go to bed. We must thank God for all he has given—"

A knock at the door interrupted her.

"Who could that be?" she wondered aloud. She opened the door to a shivering young man in a threadbare coat.

"Please, ma'am," he said, "I had very bad crops this year, and I haven't eaten in two days. Could you . . . "

"Come in, come in," Mama Margaret said. "We can always find an extra bowl of soup."

The boys looked at one another. This was not the first time this had happened, and Mama Margaret always managed to find some food for the people in need. She often gave them a place to sleep in the stable. And she always invited their "guests" to join them for the family's night prayer.

Johnny watched all of this from his place on the floor by the fireplace. From his mother's good example he was learning how to be generous and to love his neighbor. But there was much more learning to do.

The year that John turned nine, he visited one of his aunts. His aunt worked for the local priest, and the priest taught him how to read. After that, he read history books or legends aloud to his family. Sometimes other families came to listen, too. John knew that not every family prayed together like his family did. So before and after each reading, he invited his listeners to say a Hail Mary together.

In the summer, nobody wanted to be inside listening to stories. So John tried something different. During the summers when he was ten, beginning and through his teenage years, he went to watch the traveling jugglers and acrobats in town. Then he practiced and practiced: tightrope walking, leaps and cartwheels, and handstands. He learned some magic tricks, too.

For John Bosco, Sunday was show day! After Mass, he gathered the children and some of the villagers in a corner of his family's field. He jumped up on the tightrope that he had stretched between two trees.

"Before we start," he called out, "we're going to pray a Rosary."

The crowd grumbled.

"We didn't come here to pray," someone said. A few people started to leave.

"After the Rosary, we'll have the show," John said. "That's how it works." Then he started the Rosary.

As promised, after the Rosary, he jumped back up on the tightrope and began leaping, jumping, and cartwheeling.

A few Sundays later, John expanded his show . . . and the prayer time! After the Rosary, he repeated what he remembered from the homily he had heard preached at

*"After the Rosary, we'll have the show," John said.
"That's how it works."*

Mass. Then he walked through the crowd. Suddenly he pretended to pull a small rock out of a little boy's ear.

"Oh!" cried the little boy. "Where did that come from?" His mother smiled.

John pulled similar stones out of the ears of two other children. Jogging to the front of the crowd, he began juggling the rocks. He continued juggling as he jumped up on the tightrope. Letting the rocks fall to the ground, he used his feet and his hands to get across the tightrope. The show continued, delighting the villagers of Becchi.

"What will he think of next?" Mama Margaret marveled.

3
GOOD NEWS

John, Joseph, and Anthony worked hard on the farm. When John worked, he had lots of time to think. He thought as he took the cows out or as he planted or hoed. He thought about what chores he would have to do tomorrow. He thought about what tricks he would do the next Sunday. And sometimes he thought about his future.

I could be a farmer, he thought as he walked. *But I think God wants something else for me. I think he wants me to be . . . a priest! Maybe the dream I had about the boys who became lambs . . . maybe that's what it meant!*

"Mama," he said one day when he came inside, "I've been thinking . . . and I want to be a priest when I grow up."

Mama Margaret smiled. "Why is that, John?"

"Because," he replied, "on Sundays, my jumps and tricks help lots of people to pray. I could do that as a priest—I could help children to pray and love God and lead good lives."

"Well, John," Mama Margaret replied, "let's keep praying about it. If God wants it, then it will be."

John was happy with this.

Not long after, Mama Margaret had news for John when he arrived home from school.

"John, is that you?" she called when she heard him.

"Yes, Mama," he answered. "What is it?"

"I have good news for you, John. I heard from the priest at the parish in Castelnuovo today. You know that children usually have to wait until they are twelve or even fourteen to receive their first Communion. Your brother Joseph has not even received his first Communion yet."

"Yes, Mama, but I want to receive Jesus so much!" John said.

"And now you will, my dear boy," Mama Margaret said. "Father has given permission for you to receive your first Communion on Easter Sunday."

John jumped up from the floor where he was sitting. "Really, Mama?" he exclaimed. "Really?"

Mama Margaret laughed and pulled John into a hug. "Really, Johnny."

The great day arrived quickly. On March 26, 1826, John Bosco received his first Holy

Communion at the parish church of Castelnuovo. He was ten years old.

"Are you excited, John?" Joseph asked.

John nodded his head up and down. He was wearing his best Sunday pants, shirt, and coat—and a big smile!

As she watched John, Joseph, and Anthony walk into the church, Mama Margaret thought about her husband. *How he would have loved to see this day,* she thought. *But I trust he is with us from heaven.*

Mass began, and soon the great moment arrived: John received Jesus for the first time in Holy Communion. He had never been happier.

That evening, Mama Margaret prepared a special supper in honor of John's special day.

"This is the best day of your life, John," she said. "God came into your heart in a new and special way this morning. Pray to him. Promise him that you will remain good and pure. Go to confession and receive Holy Communion often. Be obedient. Stay away from companions who do not lead you to God."

John remembered these words and wrote them down. *I will always try to follow Mama's advice,* he thought. *It makes my life better.*

❖❖❖

John needed to go to school if he wanted to become a priest one day. But the Boscos were too poor to pay for school.

"Pray, John," Mama Margaret told him. "If God wants it, then it will happen."

And God did make it happen!

In April, the Boscos decided to attend the parish mission in Buttigliera (Boo-til-lee-AIR-a). They walked two miles each way, morning and evening, to attend Mass and hear homilies. It was a lot of walking, but it was a special jubilee year. This meant that the parishioners would receive special graces for attending the mission.

One evening, as they were returning from the mission, John and his family were walking beside a priest from the neighboring town of Murialdo (Moo-ree-AL-doe).

"Buona sera (BWO-nah SA-ra), young man," the priest said. "Good evening."

"Good evening, Father," John replied.

"What is your name?" the priest asked.

"John Bosco, Father."

"Well, John Bosco," the priest replied, "did you understand any of the homily this evening?"

"Oh, yes, certainly," John said.

The priest chuckled. "How much of it did you understand?"

"All of it, Father," John replied.

"All of it! Well, let's see. Repeat a few sentences from the homily for me."

John repeated every point from the homily. The priest was astonished! The people walking around them began to notice, too.

"Very good, young man," he said. "You remembered the first homily very well. But do you remember the second one?"

"I do, Father," John said. "It was about the resurrection of the body. Do you want to hear all of it, too?"

"No, no, I believe you," the priest smiled. "You have an incredible memory! Where are you from? Who are your parents?"

"I am from Becchi, Father. There is my mother," John said as he pointed to Mama Margaret a few steps behind them. "My father died when I was two."

"Do you go to school?" the priest asked.

"I did, Father. I can read and write a little. But now I've finished at the school in Becchi, and we don't have enough money for me to continue."

"But do you want to learn?"

"Oh, yes," John exclaimed.

"And why is that?" the priest continued.

17

"I want to become a priest, Father," John said. "I want to teach children to pray and love God. I want to tell them how much he loves them."

They arrived at a turn in the road, leading to the Bosco's farm.

"Good night, Father," John said.

"Wait, John," the priest said. "My name is Don Calosso (DON Cah-LOSS-o). I am a priest at Murialdo. Ask your mother if she can come see me next Sunday. I would like to speak with her."

"Yes, Don Calosso," John said. (In Italian, "Don" means "Father," so Father Calosso was called Don Calosso.)

As they walked the rest of the way home, John told Mama Margaret what Don Calosso had said.

"He wants to see me?" she asked.

"That's what he said, Mama," John replied.

They continued in silence. But both of them were thinking about Don Calosso's words. What could he want? What would it mean for the future?

4
Following God's Call

The following Sunday, Mama Margaret went to see Don Calosso. He told her how impressed he was with John's memory and with his desire to become a priest. He offered to tutor John in grammar and Latin to prepare him for the seminary. When Mama Margaret told him this, John was thrilled!

But not everything in John's life was so happy. John and his brother Joseph got along well. But he didn't get along so well with his brother Anthony. Mama Margaret was Joseph and John's mother, but she was Anthony's stepmother. Because of this, Anthony was sometimes jealous of Joseph and John. He was also jealous because John went to be tutored by Don Calosso instead of helping on the farm all day.

"John! Where have you been all day?" Anthony grumbled.

"I just came home from studying," John replied. "I'm ready to help now."

"Always at school, never on the farm," Anthony continued.

"I have to study if I want to be a priest, Anthony," said John.

"Yeah, yeah, just come help me now." Anthony stomped away.

John glanced at his mother. "What should I do, Mama?" he asked. "Anthony is never nice to me. He is always complaining and yelling at me."

Mama Margaret gave John a quick hug. "I know sometimes Anthony's behavior hurts, but right now all we can do is love him, Johnny," she said. "We have to show him how much God loves him."

John sighed. "Okay, Mama," he said. "It's hard, but I'll try."

"John!" Anthony's voice came from the field. "Hurry up!"

I can start trying right now, John thought, and smiled to himself.

John liked his lessons with Don Calosso. He learned grammar and Latin and many other things. But even more, Don Calosso showed John by example what it meant to be a prayerful, holy, kind priest.

"In six months, you will have finished this whole Latin book!" Don Calosso exclaimed at Easter. "I will have to find another book for you."

"I practice while I work on the farm," John said. "But tell me again about how you knew God wanted you to be a priest. I like to hear about that."

"Very well," Don Calosso smiled.

These were times that John treasured.

John continued his studies for almost another whole year. But his home life was not as peaceful as his studies. Anthony was still angry that John spent time studying instead of helping on the farm all day. Even though John went to work on the farm as soon as he came home from his lessons with Don Calosso, it wasn't enough for Anthony. Finally, Mama Margaret realized that something would have to change.

"John, dear," she said one February evening in 1828, "Anthony is not happy about your studies."

"I know, Mama," John replied. "But what can I do? I work on the farm as much as I can."

"I've been thinking," Mama Margaret said. "Perhaps you can go to nearby Moncucco (Mon-KOO-koh) and find work at the Moglia's (MOLE-yuh's) farm. They have a big farm and they are kind people. If they hire you, then you can save money to continue your studies later."

"If you think it is best, then I will go," John said.

The very next day, John took his books and a change of clothes and set off for Moncucco. Mr. Moglia hired him as a farmhand. John helped with all the chores on the farm, especially cleaning and tidying the stables. His week was very full, but he managed to find time in the evenings to study Latin. And there was always time for Mass on Sunday.

One Sunday, Mr. Moglia was walking out of the house when he heard laughing coming from the field behind the barn. *Who could that be?* he wondered. He walked toward the sound.

"Glory be!" Mr. Moglia whispered to himself as he rounded the corner of the barn. There was his farmhand John Bosco, standing on his head in front of a crowd of people. Mr. Moglia listened.

"Now," John said, "you've seen some entertainment—I've juggled, and now I'll show you my handstand! So tell me, who remembers the first commandment?" He walked a few steps on his hands.

"I am the Lord your God . . ." one girl spoke up.

John tumbled to his feet. "That's right!" he said. He sat down on the ground in front of his eager audience. "I am the Lord your God, and you shall not have other gods before me. This means that we must love God above everything else! And do you know why?"

John smiled at the little girl. "Because God loves us!" he said. "He loves us and he knows what is best for us. The first commandment helps us to remember that God always does what is good for us. It helps us to trust God."

A woman spoke up. "But what about when bad things happen to us?" she asked.

"We must trust God even more," John said. "Only God can bring good out of the bad things that happen."

Out of the corner of his eye, John saw Mr. Moglia. He jumped to his feet.

"Hello, Mr. Moglia," he said quickly. "We're just having a Sunday catechism lesson."

"I see that," Mr. Moglia chuckled. "Come see me when you finish."

After everyone went home, John went to see Mr. Moglia.

"Do you do this every Sunday?" Mr. Moglia asked.

"Almost every Sunday, sir," John replied. "I love to teach children how to love God."

"Why, you are not much more than a child yourself, John," his employer said.

"Maybe not, sir," John answered. "But I think God wants me to be a priest. That is why I am here working, to save money for my studies. And that is why I gather the children together on Sundays."

"And that is why you stand on your head?" Mr. Moglia smiled.

John laughed. "Yes, sir," he replied.

"Well, it costs a lot of money to study to become a priest," Mr. Moglia said. "I don't know how you'll manage it."

"Somehow I will," John said.

But later that night, John thought, *Mr. Moglia is right—it does cost a lot of money to study to become a priest. I have been here for almost two years and I don't have nearly enough. What will I do? Dear God, please help me. If you want me to be a priest, please help me!*

John's prayer was soon answered. In December of 1829, he was on his way to the field with the cows. A man in a cart was driving along the road.

"Hello, Johnny!" the man called.

John recognized him—it was his mother's brother, his Uncle Michael. "Hello, Uncle Michael!"

"Your mother told me you were working for the Moglia's. How do you like it?" he asked.

"Oh, it's fine," John said. "They are kind, but . . ."

"But what, my boy?" Uncle Michael asked.

"But I want to be a priest, Uncle Michael," John said. "So I must continue my studies. And there is no possibility of continuing them here. I'm not sure what to do."

"Leave it to me, Johnny," his kind uncle said. "I will talk to the Moglia's and to your mother. We will work something out."

Indeed, Uncle Michael did work something out. John returned to the Bosco's farm in Becchi, and he resumed his lessons with Don Calosso. Shortly after John's return home, Anthony decided to take his share of the family's money and leave home. For a time, it seemed that all was well.

❖❖❖

One day in November of 1830, John went to run an errand for Don Calosso, who was now seventy-five years old. Suddenly, he heard someone shouting his name.

"John! John Bosco!" It was the priest's neighbor.

"What is it?" he asked.

"Don Calosso has had a stroke!"

John rushed back to the priest's house. Because of the stroke, Don Calosso could no longer speak. But he gave John a key. Don Calosso gestured to John that the key would open his desk. Everything in the desk would belong to John after his death.

Two days later, the good priest died.

Inside the good priest's desk there was enough money for John to continue his education. But now John wondered what to do. He was not related to Don Calosso, and he thought that Don Calosso's relatives might want the money.

Dear God, I trust that you will provide what I need for my studies, John prayed.

When the priest's relatives arrived, John gave them the key to the desk and said nothing more about it.

Now what? Don Calosso had been the answer to John's continuing his education. But God provided, just as John had asked for in prayer. Mama Margaret discovered that the priest who ran the school in Castelnuovo also gave Latin classes.

"You could go there, John," she suggested. "But it will mean a lot of walking for you. The school is more than three miles away."

"That's all right, Mama," John said. "I don't mind walking, as long as I can continue preparing to become a priest."

"But I am afraid you will wear your shoes out, Johnny," she said. "And you know we don't have the money to buy you another pair."

"Don't worry about that, Mama," John replied, with a twinkle in his eye.

Beginning that winter, John walked three miles to school in the morning and then returned home for lunch. He walked three miles back for afternoon classes and three miles home at night. To save wear on his shoes, he walked barefoot the whole way! He only put on his shoes when he reached the edge of town.

But twelve miles every day was too much for young John. He started taking his lunch with him. Sometimes the winter weather made it too difficult to return home. On those nights, he slept on the floor at the home of a friendly family in Castelnuovo.

Finally, both Mama Margaret and John realized that he needed to find somewhere to live in Castelnuovo. A man named Roberto agreed to let John stay with him and his family.

"We will pay him with a small amount of wine, corn, and eggs from the farm," Mama Margaret explained to John.

"I will miss you, Mama," John said sadly.

"Yes, John," his mother replied, "but it is for the best. Be good and study hard . . . and above all, Johnny, love the Blessed Mother. Love her very much."

John thought about his mother's advice as he started off on his last walk from Becchi to Castelnuovo. *Help me, Blessed Mother,* he prayed. *I want to follow God's call. Help me as I take this next step!*

5
THE BEAUTIFUL LADY

"Here comes the giant!"

John heard the younger boys teasing him as he walked toward the school. At fifteen years old, he was much older and taller than the other boys at the school at Castelnuovo, and they liked to tease him about it. But John didn't mind too much. He was happy to be able to study.

Something did bother him, though. The priests in Castelnuovo were not like Don Calosso. They kept to themselves and were not very available to the students. This made John sad.

When I am a priest, he thought, *I will try not to be so reserved. I will always smile and greet people, to help them know that God loves them. I especially want to help children know that God loves them.*

Roberto (the man whose family John was staying with) was a tailor—someone who made clothes. Sometimes, in addition to what the Boscos gave Roberto from the farm, John helped with the sewing to pay for his staying there.

"John, do you have some time?" Roberto asked one evening. "I have a big order of shirts and I could use some help with sewing on the buttons."

"Yes, I can help," John said.

"You are learning a lot about being a tailor, John," said Roberto's wife.

"Yes," laughed John. "So far I can sew buttons and hem pants."

"We will have to teach you how to cut out the pants and the coats," Roberto said. "You never know, it may be useful later."

John nodded. At the time he couldn't imagine how his experience working with a tailor would be very valuable.

❖❖❖

John had hoped that the school at Castelnuovo would set him on the road to being a priest. But that year, he saw that he was not learning very much. When he went home for vacation in the summer of 1831, he spoke to Mama Margaret about it.

"I don't think I should go back to Castelnuovo, Mama," he said. "I won't learn anything new there. I just don't know where I should go next. I'm worried that I will never complete my studies to become a priest."

"We must pray, John," Mama Margaret said. "Let's pray and ask God and the Blessed Mother to show us the way."

The next morning, John came whistling into the kitchen.

"Good morning, Mama," he smiled.

"Good morning, Johnny," she said. "You seem very cheerful this morning—you were very anxious yesterday."

"I know," he said. "But now I am certain that I will be a priest. God will make a way for me to complete my studies."

"That's wonderful!" Mama Margaret said. "But what makes you so sure today?"

"I had a dream," John said. "I was in a field when I saw a beautiful lady. She was leading a large flock out to graze. She was walking toward me and calling my name.

"'Come, John,' she said. 'Do you see this flock? I am putting you in charge of it.'

"'But there are so many of them,' I protested. 'What should I do with them? I do not have any fields for them.'

"'Do not be afraid, John,' she said. 'I will look after you and help you.'

"Then she disappeared.

"So, you see, Mama," John concluded, "The Blessed Mother wants me to be a priest, and she will look after me and help me."

31

*"Come, John," she said. "Do you see this flock?
I am putting you in charge of it."*

Not long after John had this dream, Mama Margaret discovered an opportunity for John to attend the school in Chieri (Kee-AIR-ee), about twelve miles away. The school had a good reputation, and he could stay with a woman named Mrs. Matta for a very low fee if he helped out around the house.

So once again John set off on a long walk to continue his studies at a new school.

❖❖❖

John had been at the school in Chieri for about a year when he walked into the classroom for Latin class and sat down. He reached for his Latin book.

Oh, no! He looked frantically through his pile of books. He had forgotten his book. *What am I going to do?* he thought. *There is no time to run back and get it!*

The other students were already beginning to review the assignment for the day. Hoping he wouldn't be called on or caught without his book, John pulled out another book and pretended to be reading Latin while he tried to think of an explanation to give his teacher.

But some of his classmates noticed, and they began to giggle.

"What are you doing?" one of them whispered.

John kept his eyes on his book, hoping hard that the teacher would not notice. But the giggling was too loud.

"What's going on?" the teacher asked sharply. "John, stand up and translate aloud the passage that I assigned yesterday for homework."

The class gasped. By now they all knew that John did not have his Latin book.

John stood up, grasping his book. He stared at the page and took a deep breath. Then closing his eyes he began to translate, from memory, the passage his teacher had asked for.

His classmates watched him with wide eyes. When he finally paused for a breath, they applauded! The teacher looked exasperated.

"Now what?" he asked. "Why are you making all this noise?"

"Look, sir," one boy said. "Bosco doesn't have his Latin book. He translated all that from memory!"

"Hmm," said the teacher. "Continue, John."

John continued. The teacher walked toward John and saw that he really was translating from memory.

"That's enough," he said. "Class, continue with the reading. John, come to my desk."

John put down his book and walked to the teacher's desk.

"You have a good and strong memory, John," the teacher said. "This is a gift from God. Your job is to use it well, and never take it for granted."

"Yes, sir," John replied.

"And try not to forget your book again!" the teacher added.

6
The Contest

John could never remain anywhere for very long without making use of his gifts for both teaching and acrobatics. In Chieri, just like in Becchi and in Moncucco, he began gathering children and young people for Sunday catechism lessons and prayer.

This time John gave his Sunday afternoon gatherings a name: the Happiness Club. His club had only two rules: first, every member must try to behave like a good Christian; and second, every member must work hard to do his best in school.

"The third rule," explained John, "is to have fun!"

And have fun they did! Sometimes they went hiking, and other times they went berry-picking. Sometimes they walked all the way to Turin (TOUR-in), about ten miles away! Usually John entertained them with his acrobatics, juggling, and magic tricks.

Their gatherings always ended with prayer. Often they went to one of the churches in Chieri to listen to the afternoon homily (at that time many churches not only had

Mass on Sunday morning, but also a homily or instruction on Sunday afternoon).

One Sunday John noticed that not many of the boys came to church for prayer after their afternoon of fun. Curious, he found out why afterward.

"Where were you all?" he asked.

"Oh, there was a professional acrobat putting on a show! He was marvelous!" one of the boys replied.

"Hmm," John said. He wondered about the timing of the acrobat's show.

Sure enough, the next Sunday, just at the time of the afternoon homily, the acrobat started another show. Many of the boys skipped church to watch him.

What can I do? John thought. *There's no harm in the acrobat's show, but I wish he wouldn't perform just when we were going to pray on Sunday.*

Then John had an idea.

The next day he waited in the town square until he saw the acrobat.

"Excuse me, sir," he said. "I would like to challenge you to a contest!"

"A contest?" the acrobat asked. "What sort of contest?"

"Running, jumping, juggling, and climbing," John replied.

The acrobat scoffed. "You really think you can beat me in a contest of jumping or juggling?" He laughed. "Very well. You will end up humiliated and even more people will come to my show! When will this contest be?"

"On Thursday," John answered.

Both John and the acrobat spread the word about the contest that was to take place. On Thursday afternoon after school, a large crowd of boys and townspeople gathered to watch John and the acrobat compete.

"Ah! There you are," the acrobat said, grinning. "And what shall our first event be?"

"Wait a moment," John responded. "There should be some sort of prize for the winner."

The crowd grew silent to hear what the prize would be.

"If I win, you will stop performing on Sunday afternoons at the time of the afternoon homily," John said. "If you win . . . you may continue performing at that time."

"Fine," said the acrobat, certain that he would win.

"Our first event will be a race," John said. "From here to the end of town."

"Very good," the acrobat replied.

The two lined up. A man counted down, "On your mark . . . get set . . . go!" They took off! The acrobat got ahead quickly and smiled. *This is going to be easy,* he thought.

John panted behind him. *Blessed Mother . . . help . . . me!* he prayed. He wanted to win, not for himself, but to help people come to church so they could learn more about God. John ran hard! He began to overtake the acrobat and eventually passed him to win the race!

"All right," the acrobat panted when they returned to the edge of town. "You have beaten me in running. But for the next event, I choose jumping."

"Where will the jump be?" John asked.

"Right here, at this spot, over the river," the acrobat replied.

John made a face. At this particular place, the river was quite wide. Not only that, but there was a low wall on the opposite side, leaving only a narrow strip of ground between the river and the wall.

"All right," John agreed. "You go first."

The acrobat didn't waste any time. He took a running start, made a perfect leap, and landed on the narrow strip of ground between the river and the wall. The crowd applauded!

"Ha! Do better than that if you can!" he called to John.

John was already running. He jumped across the river, landed with his hands on the wall, and did a handspring to the other side of the wall. The crowd cheered wildly. He was the winner again!

"My turn," he said, coming back. He grabbed a smooth stick from the river bed and put his hat on top of it. Then he started spinning it from his hand, to his elbow, to his shoulder, across his face, and down to the other hand. He handed the stick to the acrobat.

This time it really seemed like the acrobat would beat John. He, too, spun the stick up his arm, over his neck, and across his face. But he had a rather large nose, and when the stick reached it—it crashed to the ground.

John had won the challenge yet again. But there was one event left: climbing.

"You choose the place," John said to the acrobat.

"The top of that elm tree," the man replied. "And I go first." He was already removing his coat.

He climbed skillfully and rapidly toward the top. The branches began to bend beneath his weight. The crowd gasped. He had almost reached the very last branch, and the tree was swaying from side to side. He had gone as high as it was possible to go.

The acrobat came down just as quickly, and he nodded to John. John said a quick prayer and climbed swiftly toward the top. He reached the same height that the acrobat had reached. But he had a plan. He grasped the branch with his hands, lifted his legs, and did a handstand on the branch! Now his feet were higher than the top of the tree!

The crowd cheered and clapped. John had clearly won the contest!

When John reached the ground, the acrobat sullenly grumbled, "Well, you won."

"Yes," John replied. "No more Sunday afternoon shows, all right?"

"All right," the acrobat turned to go. He was sure that now nobody would come to his shows, anyway. But suddenly he heard John speaking to everyone. What was he saying?

"Make sure you all go to this man's next show," he called to the crowd. "He is a very talented acrobat!"

John was happy. Now everyone could enjoy a good show and still come to church on Sunday afternoon.

7

A Good Friend

John spent four years studying at the school in Chieri. For the first two years he stayed at Mrs. Matta's house, and during the last two years with a baker. John helped out in the bakery just as he had helped the tailor in Castelnuovo. By doing so, he learned how to bake.

One morning John's teacher was late for class, and the students began to talk. Then they began to laugh. Soon they were playing catch with balls of paper and yelling over one another's heads. But one young man sat quietly at his desk, preparing his homework.

"What are you doing?" another boy said to him. "Leave your homework and come have some fun!"

"No, thank you," the young man said.

"What, do you think you are better than us?" the offended boy asked quickly.

"Not at all, it's just—"

The boy stopped him with a quick slap to the face. The classroom fell silent.

The young man grew red, but he did not fight back. "Is that all?" he asked. "Then please leave me alone. I forgive you."

John saw all of this. "Who is that new student?" he asked.

"His name is Luigi Comollo (Koh-MOH-loh)," the boy across the aisle said. "His uncle is a priest in one of the neighboring towns."

When class finished for the morning, John hurried to catch up with Luigi.

"My name is John Bosco," he said. "I saw what you did this morning—it was very admirable."

"It was the right thing to do," Luigi replied. "I am Luigi Comollo."

"Why did you come to study here in Chieri?" asked John.

"I want to become a priest like my uncle," Luigi answered.

They shook hands. A firm and lasting friendship began.

Luigi and John often spoke about their desire and about what it would be like to be in the seminary. They talked about the things they wanted to do when they were priests. When they were almost finished at the school in Chieri, it was time to think more seriously about entering a seminary.

John was nineteen years old now. He had grown taller. His dark hair was still curly. His brown eyes had great purpose in them, but there was always a twinkle in them, too. Even though John had grown up, he still had the same fun-loving nature—and the same desire to serve God.

"Luigi," John said one day when they were walking home from class, "I am thinking about becoming a Franciscan."

"Really?" Luigi answered. "You never mentioned that before."

"It's just that . . ." John paused, "you know I can barely afford the school here in Chieri. I will never be able to afford to study at the seminary. If I enter the Franciscan Order, they will pay for my education to become a priest." He took a deep breath. "What do you think?"

"I think we should pray about it, John," Luigi replied. "And you should talk to the priests. They will help you figure out what God wants."

A few weeks later, John and Luigi were talking again.

"Well," John sighed, "now I have spoken to two priests—the priest who hears my confessions at school, and the pastor of my parish at home. My confessor said he doesn't know what I should do. My pastor said I should not become a Franciscan. I'm confused, Luigi."

"Did you talk to your mother about it?" Luigi asked. "She is a wise woman."

"Yes—"

Suddenly, John was interrupted by a group of boys talking very loudly. John recognized them from school. They were bullies who had often mistreated Luigi.

One of them stuck out his foot as John and Luigi passed by, and tripped Luigi. John was angry. He immediately punched the boy and knocked him down

"Anybody else?" he said, looking angrily at the other boys. They helped their friend up and left hurriedly.

"John," Luigi laughed gently, "you are a good friend and very strong. But remember, God didn't give you your strength so you could knock people down. He wants you to build people up by loving and forgiving them."

John never forgot this lesson.

A few days later, Mama Margaret visited John.

"Mama!" John exclaimed. "What are you doing here? It's so far from home."

"I am here to tell you something important, John," she said. "Don Dassano (Dah-SAH-no) from our parish came to see me. He tells me that you are thinking of becoming a Franciscan."

"Yes, Mama," John replied.

"Well, my son," Mama Margaret continued, "I have only one thing to say: pray. The only thing that matters is to do what God wants. Don't worry about what we can afford and what we can't afford. Don't you remember the dream you had? If God wants it, then it will happen. Remember that."

John listened to his mother's advice. He prayed, and he spoke with a holy young priest named Don Cafasso (Kah-FAH-so).

Don Cafasso prayed with John and then told him, "You should continue with your studies and enter the seminary. And—be ready to go wherever God leads you."

John felt great peace after speaking with Don Cafasso.

Thank you, God, he prayed. *Thank you for Don Cafasso's words. Thank you for always guiding me.*

Moving from school to school during the first several years of his education, John learned to trust that God would provide a way for him to prepare for the seminary. On

October 31, 1835, John Bosco entered the seminary of his diocese at Chieri. It was an occasion of great joy, but also a little sadness. The day before he left home, many family members and friends came to say good-bye. After they left, John and Mama Margaret had a moment alone.

"John," she said, her eyes filling with tears, "when you were born, I offered you to the Blessed Mother. When you began school, I prayed to her every day for you. Now you are on your way to becoming a priest. Do not forget that you belong to the Blessed Mother. If, God willing, you do become a priest, promise me you will be a good and holy priest. Promise me you will be devoted to the Blessed Mother . . ."

She could not go on.

"Mama," John's voice choked with emotion, "Mama, I am leaving you to begin a new life. But I leave with all the advice you have always given me as well as your prayers. These are a treasure to me. Thank you, Mama."

The next day, John Bosco walked through the seminary doors. *Here I am! he thought. I really am going to become a priest!*

8

IN THE SEMINARY

"Bosco! Bosco!"

A ball flew through the air and John's fellow seminarians shouted excitedly as he ran after it. It was fast . . . but so was John! He stopped the ball and kicked it in the other direction. The seminarians cheered!

Just then one of the priests, a professor at the seminary, walked by. The students quickly became very quiet. In seminaries at John's time, it was uncommon for the priests to spend time with the students outside of class. They expected the students to be quiet and solemn much of the time.

"I don't mind being quiet when we study or when we pray," John said after the priest walked by. "But I don't understand why we always have to be quiet when the priests are around."

"Yes," another seminarian agreed, "sometimes it makes me think about whether I really want to be a priest or not."

"Oh, not me!" John exclaimed. "When I am a priest, young people will never have to be quiet around me. I will play ball with them!"

John was a good student and enjoyed his classes at the seminary. He often thought about how he would use what he was learning to help people after he was ordained. During the summers, John went home. Sometimes he stayed with Mama Margaret or his brother Joseph, and he helped on the farm. But more often he stayed with the priests at Castelnuovo and helped at St. Andrew the Apostle parish. He wanted to learn as much as he could about what it was like to live as a priest. The priests there welcomed him.

"I heard you were the winner of a race today, John," one of the priests said to him at supper one evening. He winked.

John blushed. "Umm, y-y-es," he stuttered.

"What's this?" "What happened?" the others asked with curiosity.

"Ah, well . . ." John paused awkwardly.

The first priest came to his rescue. "John beat a rabbit in a race this morning!"

The other priests looked at each other and then burst out laughing.

"A rabbit—whatever for?" one of them asked.

John joined in the laughter. "I was outside studying when I saw the rabbit hop by," he explained. "And I wondered if I was fast enough to catch it. It turns out I was!"

John enjoyed these times of laughter and conversation with the priests in Castelnuovo. He also enjoyed serving at Mass for them, and watching how they took care of people. Staying with them gave John the opportunity to ask them questions about what it was like to be a priest.

There were many books at the parish, and the priests let John borrow them to continue studying during the summer. One year he tutored some of the other seminarians in Greek. Another time he taught Latin and literature.

John's summer students even came to the seminary during the year to ask him for help or advice. These students started to spread the word about John. "He is fun to be with," they told their friends. "He talks about God, but he talks about other things, too, like juggling and sports."

"It is easy to ask him questions," others said. "He always finds out the answers for us."

On Sundays when school was in session, the seminarians walked from the seminary to the cathedral for Mass. Sometimes these students would wait along the way just to wave to John or point him out to their friends.

"See him?" they said. "He is a friend to all of us."

That is what I want to be, John thought—*a friend to all of you.*

John's fellow seminarians knew they could count on him, too.

"Did you understand the lecture this morning?" one seminarian asked another after class.

"Not too well," the other replied. "If you want, you can come with me this afternoon. Bosco is going to explain it to me. He always helps me when I don't understand."

"Yes," another seminarian added, "he helped me with Latin once."

"And he helped me mend my cassock when I tore it playing ball!" yet another said.

John's closest friend growing up, Luigi Comollo, was also at the seminary in Chieri. He and John had many long talks about the priesthood and what they hoped to do to help young people know more about God.

"Only heaven is important," Luigi said one day when they were taking a walk.

"Yes, only heaven," John agreed. "That is what we have to tell people."

"But we have to remember it ourselves, too," Luigi said. "Listen, John, let's make a promise. Probably we will not die for a very long time. But let's promise that whichever one of us dies first will send some sort of sign to show that he is in heaven. A sign like that would encourage the one of us who is still here."

"Of course, Luigi, I'll be happy to hear from you, especially after you've died!" John said, chuckling. *That won't happen for a long time, John thought.*

Sadly, however, during their fourth year at the seminary, Luigi became very sick. He had a high fever, but the doctor could not diagnose what was wrong with him. John went to see him every day and spent many hours with him.

On Holy Saturday, Luigi's fever became even worse. He was restless, and sometimes John had to stop him from getting out of bed. Luigi was becoming sicker and sicker. The priest came to give him the Anointing of the Sick and Holy Communion. John could hardly believe what was happening. It seemed his best friend was dying.

On April 3 of 1839, the Tuesday after Easter, John was praying with Luigi. After Luigi received Holy Communion, he became very peaceful and then quietly died. John felt both sad and distressed.

"I don't know what to think," John kept saying to Mama Margaret. "He was my best friend."

"He will still be your best friend," Mama Margaret replied. "Now he is your best friend in heaven."

While John's faith was strong, he felt shaken. But the night after Luigi's funeral, something unusual happened. All of the seminarians were in bed when a loud rumbling sound filled the dormitory. It sounded like a train was going through their hallway!

All of the seminarians got out of bed and came into the hall. What was going on?

As the rumbling sounded faded away, the seminarians heard a voice. It repeated three times, "Bosco, I am in heaven." Then a bright light filled the hallway.

John understood immediately that Luigi was keeping the promise he had made to give him a sign that he was in heaven! Great peace filled John's heart.

"It's all right," he reassured the other terrified seminarians. "It's Luigi. He is in heaven and now he is praying for us."

That wasn't the only unusual thing that happened to John before he became a priest. One night when he was home for the summer, Mama Margaret heard him having a long and prayerful conversation with someone in his bedroom.

"Who were you talking with so long last night?" she asked him in the morning.

"With Luigi Comollo," John replied.

He didn't have to say anything more. Mama Margaret knew that Luigi was being John's best friend from heaven!

9
Don Bosco

John walked slowly into the kitchen. It was the summer before his final year at the seminary and he was home for a few days.

"Mama," he said, almost like a question.

"What is it, Johnny?" she asked.

"I had another dream last night," he said. "It seemed as if I were on Joseph's farm. But suddenly the farm became a large city filled with many people. There were many young people in the streets. At first I thought they were laughing and playing. But as I walked among them, I could hear them shouting and cursing.

"They wouldn't stop, so I began to shout at them. Then I began to strike them to make them stop. It didn't work—they hit me back and I had to run.

"Suddenly I bumped into a man who told me to go back to the young people. I showed him my cuts and bruises where the young people had hit me. The man showed me a beautiful lady.

"'This is my mother,' he said. 'Do as she advises you.'

"The lady looked at me kindly. 'You cannot teach these young people to be good by hitting and kicking them,' she said gently. 'You must capture them with gentleness and kindness.'

"Remember my first dream, Mama?" John concluded. "The boys turned into wild beasts, and then into little lambs."

"I remember," Mama Margaret replied softly.

"The same thing happened in this dream," John said. "I'm sure God wants me to be a priest and to do something with young people. God wants to use me to tell young people about his love. But I must do it with gentleness and kindness."

❖❖❖

On the Saturday before Palm Sunday in 1841, John became a deacon. This was the last step before he would become a priest. One day after Easter, there was an announcement.

"In a few weeks, you will begin your retreat," the priest in charge of the seminary said. "This will be a time of silence and prayer for you to prepare for your ordination to the priesthood."

John and his classmates looked at one another excitedly. It was really happening!

They began their retreat on May 26, 1841. John spent a lot of time in chapel praying. *God,* he prayed, *I want to help young people to know you and show them how to love you. Blessed Mother, I belong to you. Make me a good priest.*

John thought intently about how he wanted to live as a priest. At the end of the retreat, John wrote several statements in a notebook. *God has blessed me during this retreat,* he thought as he wrote. *He has invited me to try to be a good and holy priest. This is how I want to live.*

Among other things, John wrote: "I will use my time well.

"I will be ready to make sacrifices so that many people can know God.

"I will be satisfied with the food set before me, even if I do not like it.

"I will work hard.

"I will take some time every day for meditation and spiritual reading.

"Every day I will visit Jesus in the Blessed Sacrament.

"I will always take time to pray before Mass and after Mass.

"I will try to be charitable and gentle, like Saint Francis de Sales."

Saint Francis de Sales was one of John's favorite saints. Two hundred years before, Francis had been the bishop of Geneva, Switzerland. Because Geneva was just over one hundred miles away, Saint Francis de Sales was well-known and loved by many people in the region of Italy around Turin. John admired the holy bishop for how he explained the Catholic faith, and for his gentleness and joy.

On Saturday, June 5, 1841, Archbishop Luigi Fransoni, the archbishop of Turin, ordained John Bosco a priest.

The archbishop laid his hands on John's head and prayed to the Holy Spirit. Now John was Father Bosco. From now on, the people he served would call him "Don Bosco."

The next day was Trinity Sunday. This is the day when the Church celebrates the mystery of the Holy Trinity: God the Father, God the Son, and God the Holy Spirit. On this day, in the church of St. Francis of Assisi in Turin, Don Bosco celebrated his first Mass. His friend Don Cafasso was there with him.

As Don Bosco prayed the prayers of the Mass, he thought about all his studies. He remembered how hard it was to find the right school. He thought about all the generous people who had helped him along the way and about those who had taught him their skills. He prayed for all these people, especially for his childhood parish priest Don Calosso. He also prayed for his best friend Luigi. How John wished that the two of them had been ordained together!

Don Bosco remembered all his dreams, too. He thought about all the people God was calling him to serve.

Young people, he thought. *God wants me to help young people.*

And, of course, he remembered the good advice he had received from his mother. "Promise me you will be devoted to the Blessed Mother," Mama Margaret had said all those years ago.

In order to thank his Heavenly Mother for helping him on the way, John wanted his second Mass to be at a church dedicated to the Blessed Mother. So the next day he celebrated his Mass at the Church of Our Lady of Victories in Turin.

Finally, John came back to Castelnuovo. On the feast of Corpus Christi (the Body and

Blood of Christ), he celebrated Mass and led the Eucharistic procession. The day ended with a festival of food and music. Everyone was so happy!

That evening, Don Bosco and Mama Margaret walked home from the church.

"We have walked this road together so many times, Mama," Don Bosco said.

"It's true," Mama Margaret agreed. "But we have never walked it like this. Now you are a priest!"

"I can hardly believe it," Don Bosco said. "I am a priest. I can offer the Mass. I can hear confessions. I can help lead people to God."

"Yes, you can offer Mass," Mama Margaret said. "Now you will pray the Mass every day. But remember, Johnny, beginning to pray Mass means beginning to suffer."

"What do you mean, Mama?" Don Bosco asked. "I have never been so happy as I am when I celebrate Mass."

"You will be happy, Johnny. But you will also suffer. Jesus suffered and you will, too. But remember that I am always praying for you. Pray for me, too, won't you?"

"Of course, Mama," Don Bosco replied. "I will pray for you at every Mass. I always pray for you and think of you."

"Yes, pray for me, Johnny," Mama Margaret said. "And I will pray for all the souls God wants to touch through you. God wants to use you to bring many souls to him. Always remember that."

They reached home. John went to his room.

Now I am a priest, he thought. *My whole life has led to this moment. Thank you, God! Thank you, Blessed Mother!*

He took off the Roman collar that priests wore and looked at it.

I wonder what is next for me, he thought. *I have so many ideas, so many dreams. But what does God want? Where will he lead me next?*

10
THE BEGINNING

In Italy at this time, many men were becoming priests. After a man became a diocesan priest, there were several options for what type of work he would do. Some priests worked in parishes. Others worked in schools, at seminaries, in hospitals, or as chaplains in private homes.

Sometimes a new priest's assignment came from the bishop. But sometimes a school, a home, or a parish would offer work to a new priest.

After his ordination, Don Bosco wondered what type of work he would do. Again he asked advice from his friend Don Cafasso.

"I am ready to begin serving God's people!" he told Don Cafasso. "It's so exciting to think about the many things I can do to help people to come closer to God."

"Yes, it is exciting," Don Cafasso said. "Have you thought about coming to the Ecclesiastical College in Turin where I teach? Many young priests come there for extra training after their ordination."

"The Ecclesiastical College?" Don Bosco hesitated. "But I just finished at the seminary. I don't think I want to keep going to school; I want to start working for God!"

"Of course!" said Don Cafasso. "At the Ecclesiastical College, though, classes are held only in the mornings. In the afternoons you will help in the local parishes, hospitals, prisons, and schools."

"But why shouldn't I go directly to serving in the parishes and schools?" Don Bosco asked.

"Sometimes the first years of priesthood are difficult," Don Cafasso explained. "At the seminary the schedule is very structured. Sometimes it is hard to adjust to life as a priest. The Ecclesiastical College is a combination of seminary life and priestly life. If you come, you will learn how to live your life as a priest in a good and holy way."

"Well, maybe that's a good idea," Don Bosco agreed. "I will pray about it."

Don Bosco did pray about it. He felt that God was inviting him, through Don Cafasso, to attend the Ecclesiastical College. In the mornings he attended classes. In the afternoons he visited the families of Turin to pray with them and encourage them. Every day he prayed with the other young priests.

He knew he was in the right place.

❖❖❖

"Don Cafasso, I am worried," Don Bosco came to his mentor only a few weeks after he arrived at the college.

"What is it, Don Bosco?" Don Cafasso asked.

"You know that in the afternoons I have been visiting the families in Turin," Don Bosco said.

"Yes, of course."

"It's terrible!" Don Bosco exclaimed. "These families are so poor—often eight or ten people live in one room. The children don't go to school. They are on the street all day, sometimes begging, sometimes encouraging bad habits in one another. Many of them steal and lie and . . . and the gangs!"

Don Cafasso nodded his head with concern.

"Only a few days ago I was walking through the streets," Don Bosco continued. "There were several groups of boys all over the city. Some were fighting, some were gambling, others were cursing. I tried to speak to them, but it's no use! Some of them ran away, but others just stood there and ignored me."

As he spoke, Don Bosco recalled his dream. *These boys are like wild beasts,* he thought to himself. *Does God want me to help turn them into lambs? I must pray to the Blessed Mother. She will help me.*

Don Bosco continued studying, but each afternoon he walked through Turin and visited homes. He asked the Blessed Mother to show him what to do about what he saw.

December 8, 1841 was the feast of Mary's Immaculate Conception. Don Bosco went to the sacristy of the church of St. Francis of Assisi to prepare for Mass.

The door of the sacristy opened onto the street. It was slightly open because Don Bosco was waiting for the altar server. The server hadn't come yet, so Don Bosco sat down and closed his eyes to pray.

A boy about fifteen or sixteen years old quietly pushed the door open and crept into the sacristy. Don Bosco was still praying and didn't notice him.

Just then, a man who had been setting up for Mass came into the sacristy.

"What are you doing here?" he said roughly. "Are you here to serve Mass?"

"N-n-no," the boy stammered.

"Then get out of here! The priest is waiting to begin Mass." The man grabbed a broom and started to chase the boy out.

"What are you doing?" Don Bosco demanded. "Why are you treating my friend like that?"

"This is your friend?" the man asked.

"Anyone who is treated badly is my friend," Don Bosco said. "Come here," he turned to the boy. "What is your name?"

"Bartholomew . . . Bartholomew Garelli (Gah-RELL-ee)."

"Where are you from, Bartholomew?"

"I am from Asti (AH-stee), but I live in Turin now," Bartholomew replied.

"Are you parents here, too?" Don Bosco asked.

"My parents are dead."

"Ah, I'm sorry," Don Bosco said. "How old are you?"

"Sixteen."

"Can you read and write?"

"No," Bartholomew answered with embarrassment. He hung his head.

"What about singing or whistling?"

Bartholomew laughed. He liked this priest.

Now Don Bosco knew Bartholomew felt more comfortable. So he asked, "Have you made your first Communion?"

"Not yet, Father," Bartholomew replied.

"Have you been to confession?"

"Oh, yes, but it was a long time ago."

Don Bosco continued to ask questions. He discovered that Bartholomew had once learned his prayers, but he had forgotten them. He went to Mass almost every Sunday, but he didn't go to catechism lessons because he was ashamed that the younger boys knew more than he did.

"If I taught you catechism, would you come?" Don Bosco asked.

"Sure," Bartholomew said.

"Very good," Don Bosco said. "We will begin as soon as I finish saying Mass."

After Mass, Don Bosco prayed a quick Hail Mary to ask the Blessed Mother for help. He joined Bartholomew in the sacristy and taught him the Sign of the Cross.

"Now, you will come back on Sunday, won't you?" he asked when they finished.

"Yes, I will!" Bartholomew said.

"Good," Don Bosco replied. "I'll see you Sunday then . . . and bring your friends."

The next Sunday, there were nine boys in the sacristy, relearning their prayers with

Don Bosco. They came back the following week, too.

A few weeks later, Don Bosco was leaving the church on Sunday evening. He noticed a few young boys sleeping in the back of the church.

"What are you doing there, my friends?" he asked with a smile.

The boys looked at each other. Then one of them spoke up.

"We came for the afternoon homily," he said. "But it didn't make any sense to us."

"Come with me," Don Bosco said. He led them to the sacristy where twelve other boys were waiting for Don Bosco to teach them about God. Every week, the number of boys who came grew larger.

A few months later, Don Bosco went to see Don Cafasso.

"Father, I need your advice," he said. "I began with one boy. That turned into twelve, and then eighty, and now there are more than one hundred! We have to meet in the churchyard because the sacristy is too small, but even the churchyard is not large enough for so many boys. What can I do?"

"We will put them in the courtyard at the Ecclesiastical College," Don Cafasso said. "God is sending these boys to you."

"God is sending these boys to you."

"He is indeed," Don Bosco replied. *And only God knows where this will go!* he added to himself.

11
THE "FLYING ORATORY"

"Catch!" Don Bosco called. A ball went flying through the air and a boy on the opposite side of the yard caught it.

"Bravo!" Don Bosco laughed. "Good job!"

He walked away to prepare for his afternoon homily, leaving the boys to their games. *How much our group has grown in three years,* he thought. *Now there are close to three hundred boys, and we have an even bigger place for our gatherings.*

It was now 1844, and Don Bosco was at St. Philomena's Refuge, an orphanage started and run by a wealthy woman, Lady di Barolo (Bah-ROE-loe). Don Bosco helped Don Borel (Bo-RELL), who was the chaplain of the orphanage. They took care of the spiritual needs of the children there.

When Don Bosco started helping at the orphanage in 1844, he asked Don Borel and Lady Barolo if he could use part of the building for his group of boys. The group had grown tremendously. Most of the boys were workers or apprentices. They had come to the city to learn a job. Some of them had come to earn money to support their families who lived in the country. Some of them had no family. But none of them were paid much, and they often lived in very poor places.

At St. Philomena's Refuge there was a large empty room that they met in for teaching and for games, and a living room that they used as a chapel.

Don Bosco blessed the rooms on December 8, 1844—exactly three years after he met Bartholomew Garelli in the sacristy of St. Francis of Assisi. He named it the Oratory of St. Francis de Sales.

"We will call it an 'oratory,' just like Saint Philip Neri called the groups he used to gather together in Rome for catechism lessons," Don Bosco told Don Borel. "The oratory will be a place for boys to pray, learn—and play," Don Bosco explained.

"And why do you want to name it after Saint Francis de Sales?" Don Borel asked.

"Ah!" Don Bosco replied. "I have a special devotion to Saint Francis de Sales and often ask him to pray for me and for my work."

Don Borel nodded.

"I believe that Saint Francis de Sales will help us teach these boys, not only because he was such a good teacher, but also because he believed that anyone could become holy," Don Bosco continued. "Saint Francis de Sales was known for his gentleness and love. His example will help us to show the boys how much God loves them."

❖❖❖

Unfortunately, the Oratory of St. Francis de Sales did not stay at St. Philomena's Refuge for very long.

"Don Bosco," Lady Barolo called, her dress swishing down the hallway. "Don Bosco!"

Don Bosco poked his head out of a door. "Lady Barolo," he said, "how can I help you?"

"Don Bosco, this is unacceptable. Simply unacceptable!"

"What is it?" Don Bosco asked.

"Your boys make so much noise when they are here on Sundays," Lady Barolo sputtered. "The neighbors are complaining. The boys are always running around and climbing trees, and now—oh! And now!"

Don Bosco couldn't imagine what else had happened.

"They have trampled the gardens, Don Bosco. Some of the roses have disappeared.

The rest are completely ruined!" she exclaimed.

Don Bosco could see that Lady Barolo was very upset. He tried to calm her. "Now, Lady Barolo," he said, "you know the boys didn't mean any harm. They are just . . ."

"You and your unruly boys must leave!" Lady Barolo interrupted.

"What?" Don Bosco asked.

"You must leave," she repeated. "It is too much. You may not meet here at my orphanage any longer."

So Don Bosco immediately began to search for a new place where the Oratory of St. Francis de Sales could meet. Soon he found a chapel next to a cemetery, surrounded by many fields. The old priest at the chapel was happy to let Don Bosco and the boys use both the chapel and the fields.

But the very next week, the same thing happened. The boys were too loud and too mischievous, and they were told to leave. Don Bosco talked to the boys about being quiet and respectful.

Still, he thought to himself, *I can't expect them to be quiet all the time! I want to give them a place where they can play and laugh, even if it is noisy!*

For months Don Bosco and his boys kept moving around. Sometimes neighbors complained about the noise—and the oratory had to move again. At other times the building was not big enough—and the oratory had to move. At times there was no building, so they gathered outside. But once the weather turned cold—the oratory had to move again.

"Boys!" Don Bosco called one Sunday afternoon. "I have an announcement for you."

"Are we moving again?" one of the boys asked immediately.

Don Bosco laughed. "You guessed it! We are moving again. But this time I have invented something to make the moving easier."

The boys looked around at one another. A new invention? What was Don Bosco talking about?

"The invention is called . . . the flying oratory!" Don Bosco said. "Every Sunday, we will gather at a different place. It will be up to you to spread the word about where our meeting places will be."

So the "flying oratory" took off. Each Sunday, at the end of the day's games, catechism lessons, confessions, and prayer, Don

Bosco announced where the next Sunday's meeting place would be.

One day, Don Bosco went to visit Don Borel.

"How is your 'flying oratory'?" Don Borel asked.

"Well, it is still flying," Don Bosco replied. "We are still gathering every Sunday. And we gather on some evenings during the week, too. But it is not easy. We need a permanent place."

"Permanent?" said Don Borel. "You know what some of the other priests of Turin are saying, don't you?"

"What is that?" asked Don Bosco.

"They think that these boys should attend their own parishes instead of gathering with you every Sunday."

"But until they started gathering with me, they weren't going to church!" Don Bosco exclaimed. "They don't even know which parishes they belong to."

"You are right," Don Borel replied. "But you need to know what people are thinking and how they feel about your rowdy boys."

"That is why we need a permanent place," Don Bosco continued. "In my mind, I can see it. We will have churches, fields, playgrounds, and workplaces. There will be many priests and teachers helping to care for the boys. And we will have hundreds, maybe even thousands of children . . ."

Don Borel looked worried. "My dear Don Bosco, you have nothing right now. How can you say that you will have all of this?"

"I don't know how," Don Bosco answered, "but I know that we will have it. God and the Blessed Mother will make it so."

"You have big dreams, Don Bosco," Don Borel said, shaking his head and smiling.

When some of the other priests in Turin heard of Don Bosco's dreams, they did more than shake their heads. They did not think that this was a good plan. Some even tried to think of a way to stop him.

Two men came to question Don Bosco about his plans. Don Bosco told them all about the churches, playgrounds, teachers, and children he would have in the future. When the men left, they said to each other, "He's crazy! He belongs in an institution for people who have mental problems."

These men told two priests from Turin about their conversation with Don Bosco. A few days later, these two priests went to visit him. Don Bosco told them about his plans, too. When he finished, one priest looked at the other and nodded. The second priest said, "Don Bosco, would you like to go for a little drive in the carriage with us?"

Don Bosco looked at the priests, suspecting something.

"Of course, Fathers," he said. "Just a moment—I will get my hat."

They went outside, where the carriage was waiting. Don Bosco opened the carriage door and waved the two priests in.

"After you, Fathers," he said politely. The priests got into the carriage. Don Bosco slammed the door shut!

"Quick, to the institution!" he said to the driver. As the carriage sped off, Don Bosco prayed silently, *Lord, forgive me! I'm just trying to get rid of them. I don't mean them any harm.*

When the carriage reached the institution for people with mental problems, the doctors there soon realized that Don Bosco had tricked the two priests. No one ever tried to put Don Bosco in an institution again.

12
WILL HE LIVE?

For two years, the flying oratory met in different places. The number of boys who came each Sunday continued to grow.

What am I going to do? Don Bosco thought. *I have four hundred boys now and nowhere to gather them. Blessed Mother, help me. . . .*

"Come, boys," he said the next Sunday. "We are going to the shrine of Our Lady of the Fields. I have something to ask the Blessed Mother for, and you are going to ask for it with me."

As Don Bosco led the boys to the shrine, he noticed people staring at them.

We must be quite a sight, he smiled to himself. He knew that many people disapproved of what he was doing. He was not even sure what his own family thought about it. But Don Bosco had never been more convinced that this was what God wanted him to do.

When they arrived at the shrine, Don Bosco led all the boys in a prayer to the Blessed Mother. The boys did not know exactly what they were asking for, but they could see that Don Bosco was worried.

They finished their prayers and went back to playing. Don Bosco watched them. So many boys! So many souls! *Where will we meet next Sunday?* he prayed. *Dear God, are you asking us to stop these gatherings? What should we do?*

Suddenly, a stranger approached and asked, "Are you Don Bosco?"

"I am," Don Bosco replied.

"I hear you are looking for a place for your boys to gather," the man said.

Don Bosco smiled. "Yes, I am," he said.

"I have a friend who owns a barn in a field. He wants to rent it. Are you interested?"

Of course Don Bosco was interested. He prayed a Rosary of thanksgiving with the boys that night. The next week he made an agreement to rent Mr. Pinardi's (Pih-NAR-dee) barn and field for the year. The Pinardi House became the first permanent Oratory of St. Francis de Sales.

Now that the oratory had a permanent place, Don Bosco knew he needed to work there full time. Up until 1846, he had been working at St. Philomena's Refuge during the week and meeting with the boys from the oratory in the evenings and on weekends. He also preached, heard confessions in the parishes, and visited people in hospitals and prisons. His hard work and long hours made him very, very tired. In July of 1846, all this work caught up with him.

"Help! Help!" one of the boys called. Several other boys came running over.

"What is it?"

"Don Bosco—he fainted!" the boy said.

"Go get the bigger boys," one boy took charge. "We must carry him to bed. Then go find Don Borel or another priest."

When the doctor came, he saw that Don Bosco had severe pneumonia. His fever got worse during the week. The following week, Don Borel came to give him the sacrament of Anointing of the Sick. Mama Margaret and Joseph came. Everyone was afraid he might die.

The boys took turns keeping watch outside Don Bosco's door. They prayed Rosary after Rosary. They took turns staying in church, asking the Blessed Mother to save Don Bosco's life.

"Tonight is the most important night," the doctor said one evening. "Tonight we will see if Don Bosco lives or dies."

Don Borel was in the room. He sat beside Don Bosco's bed.

"Don Bosco," he whispered. "Don Bosco, can you hear me?"

Don Bosco nodded.

"All your boys are praying for you," Don Borel said. "They need you. I think God needs you to look after them."

"God's will be done," Don Bosco whispered.

"Yes, but let's pray," Don Borel said. "Repeat these words after me: Lord, if it is your will, heal me. I ask you this for the sake of all your children."

Don Bosco repeated the words. Don Borel smiled.

"We have all been praying for this," he said. "But now you have asked for it, too. Now I am sure that you will be healed."

The next morning the doctor was amazed by Don Bosco's improvement. "He will live," he said. "The worst is over, and he will live."

Don Bosco returned home to Becchi after his illness to rest. In the meantime, Don Borel and some other friends took care of the oratory.

"You were very sick, Johnny," Mama Margaret said one day.

"Yes, Mama," Don Bosco said. "Do you know why I think God healed me?"

"Why is that?" Mama Margaret asked.

"I think God wants me to continue his work at the oratory," Don Bosco answered. "God will help the oratory grow. He will use me to help many boys. I want to spend the rest of my life helping these boys, Mama. I really care about them."

Don Bosco stayed in Becchi resting and recovering for a few months. In the meantime, the oratory was growing. They rented four more rooms on land owned by Mr. Pinardi. But now Don Bosco had a problem. These rooms were in a rough part of town, where crimes often occurred. Don Bosco needed someone to live with him at the oratory, so that people wouldn't think that he was doing bad things.

He talked over his problem with the pastor in Castelnuovo.

"Yes, you need someone to live there with you," the pastor said. "Someone with great virtue and a holy character. Why don't you ask your mother?"

"My mother?" said Don Bosco. "I hadn't thought of that. I don't know . . . she is older now. Perhaps she doesn't want to live in a place where four or five hundred young boys come every week. Perhaps all that commotion would be too much for her."

When he went home, he watched his mother move around the kitchen making dinner. For so long she had given of herself for others. He wasn't sure if he should ask her about moving in with him. But he didn't know how he could do it all without her, either.

"Mama," he began.

"Yes, John," she said. She picked up a long wooden spoon and stirred the soup she was making.

"Would you come to live with me at the oratory?"

Mama Margaret turned around. "At the oratory? Whatever for, John?"

"I need someone like you, Mama," he said. "I need someone holy who will be a good example for the people living around us. I need someone who will be gentle with the boys and like a mother to them. And . . . I need someone to be there to support me."

Mama Margaret paused. She loved her son very much. She loved God very much, too.

"If you are asking me, then it must be because you have prayed about it," she said, "and because you think it is God's will. If it is God's will, then I will come."

Don Bosco had come to Becchi alone to recover from his illness. On November 3, 1846, he returned to Turin and to the oratory not only healed, but also with a "mother" for all the boys there.

13

A Special Project

"We are going to be like honeybees," Don Bosco announced to the boys one Sunday.

They all looked at one another. Bees? What is Don Bosco talking about? Even Mama Margaret did not know what he meant.

"When a beehive becomes too small for all the bees to fit, some of the bees go to start another hive," Don Bosco explained. "Well, our 'hive' is too small for all of us. So we are going to start another oratory!"

In fact, in the next three years Don Bosco started three more oratories in and around Turin. He could not personally visit all the oratories every Sunday. But he had a plan for this, too! He was already giving evening classes to the boys in catechism, reading, writing, grammar, and arithmetic. Now he asked some of the boys who were very good in class to come for extra classes. He trained them to help teach the other boys.

Up to this time, the oratories had been a place for hundreds of boys to gather on Sundays. They played together, learned the catechism, ate, and prayed. During the week, they went back to their homes and their jobs. Some of them, however, did not have homes; they went back to the streets where they lived.

One night in May of 1847, Don Bosco and his mother were getting ready for bed when they heard a knock on the door.

"Who could that be?" Mama Margaret exclaimed. "It's pouring rain out there!"

Don Bosco opened the door. A young boy was there.

"E-excuse me," he said. "The boys on the street said I could come here. I have no mother or father, and I came to Turin to look for work. But I haven't found a job yet, and now I am cold and hungry and—"

"Come in!" Don Bosco said warmly.

Mama Margaret was already stirring up the fire and warming some soup and bread.

"We will put some blankets in the kitchen, and you can sleep there," she said.

Word spread, and soon another boy came to sleep at the oratory. Then another, and another!

"John," said Mama Margaret, "it is wonderful that these boys have a warm place to sleep now. But we are running out of room!"

"I know, Mama," Don Bosco answered. "I have a meeting with Mr. Pinardi tomorrow. He owns this land and this house. Maybe he will sell it to us."

❖❖❖

"Of course I will sell it to you," Mr. Pinardi said the next day. "I told you before. I will sell it for three thousand livres." (That's about $44,000 by today's standards.)

"And I told you last year, and the year before," Don Bosco replied, "even though it is a generous offer, I cannot afford three thousand livres."

"What can you afford?" Mr. Pinardi asked.

"I can afford one thousand," Don Bosco answered.

"Only one thousand, eh?" Mr. Pinardi thought about it. "Well, if you pay it all in cash, then I will sell it to you for one thousand."

"Done!" said Don Bosco.

He went back to the oratory and told Mama Margaret.

"But John!" she cried. "Where will you get the money? We don't have anything!"

"Don't worry, Mama," he said. "If you had money, you would give me some, right?"

"Of course," she replied.

"Well, God is even more generous than you are," he said smiling, "and he will provide the money we need."

God did provide. That week, two people came to Don Bosco with donations of money that added up to 1,000 livres. On February 19, 1851, Don Bosco became the owner of the Pinardi House, and he officially named it the Oratory of St. Francis de Sales.

❖❖❖

An idea began to form in Don Bosco's mind and heart. He couldn't tell anyone about it yet, but he believed that God had a big plan for his oratories, that they would one day go beyond Turin and even beyond Italy. Don Bosco needed helpers.

God does not want me to do this all by myself, he thought. *He wants many people to help me. Dear God, you are beginning something new in this work. Show me which of the boys you are calling to be part of this special mission.*

Already Don Bosco was teaching many of the older boys so that they could help him to teach at the oratories. Now he began to teach these boys less about arithmetic and more about God. He taught them about prayer, about the Church and the Bible, and even about the priesthood. He talked to them about the oratories and the direction it seemed God was leading him to take.

"I believe that God wants these oratories to spread throughout Italy, and continue into the future, so that many boys will be helped," he said. He watched their eyes. "And I believe that God is calling some of you to assist me. What do you think?"

Don Bosco noticed that a few of the boys seemed especially excited when he said this: Michael Rua (ROO-ah), John Cagliero (Cah-lee-AIR-oh), Joseph Rocchietti (Roh-KYET-tee), and one or two others.

Don Bosco spoke with this small group of boys after the conference. "How would you boys like to begin classes in Latin?" Because only seminarians and priests studied Latin at that time, it was as if Don Bosco was asking them if they wanted to become priests. Michael Rua spoke up right away.

"I would like that very much, Don Bosco," he said. "I think God is calling me to help you in this work."

The other boys agreed. That week Don Bosco sent them to a school in Turin to begin Latin classes.

A few months later, on the evening of June 5, 1852, Don Bosco gathered with these boys and a few others as usual. But tonight Don Bosco had something different to tell them.

"Tonight," he began, "we are not going to speak about Latin, or about prayer, or about the Bible. Tonight I want to tell you what I believe God wants for us and for the oratories."

Don Bosco was excited and spoke quickly. "God wants us to work together. As priests and seminarians, we will dedicate ourselves to God for the purpose of taking care of young people."

"But how are we going to do this?" one of them asked.

"We'll do what we're already doing here at the oratory," he answered. "Our mission will be to take care of young people all over the world! We will look after their physical needs and educate them, yes. But we will especially look after their spiritual needs."

One after another they responded.

"Count me in!"

"And me!"

"When can we begin?"

14

An Important Step

"What is it like at the oratory? What do you do there?"

Over and over, in the streets of Turin, boys spread the word that they had found a safe place to stay: the Oratory of St. Francis de Sales.

"We pray morning prayer, and then Don Bosco says Mass for us. And he is always ready to hear our confessions or talk with us," one boy said.

"Mama Margaret—that's Don Bosco's mother—cooks breakfast for us. We all help with the dishes," another chimed in.

"But what do you do during the day? I have a job. I can't spend all day there," one boy said. He was interested in the oratory, but he wasn't sure if he wanted to live there.

"Some of us have jobs, too," the first boy said. "We go to work during the day. But we can come back to the oratory for lunch. And the boys who don't have jobs go to school."

"We come back to the oratory for supper, too," the second boy finished. "And we pray evening prayer. And guess what we do every night?"

"What?"

"Every night Don Bosco gives us a few good thoughts to think about as we go to sleep. It's a tradition!"

"Sounds like a lot of praying," the other boy said, unsure of how he felt about that.

"Maybe," the first boy said, "but we have fun, too! On Sundays we play games all afternoon. And Don Bosco plays with us!"

Boys kept coming to the oratory. Every week there were more.

Again, Mama Margaret said to her son, "John, we are running out of room!"

In July of 1852, construction began on the land next to the oratory. It was a long time before the new building was finished. Floods destroyed it once, and Don Bosco kept running out of money. But finally, in October of 1853, the new oratory was finished.

It was big enough for sixty-five boys to live in—and it immediately filled up! Soon buildings were added to the right and to the left, including a chapel. The buildings were always full of boys who had no other place to live and wanted to stay at the oratory.

At first the boys went to school or work in Turin and came home to the oratory to eat, pray, play, and sleep. But soon Don Bosco thought, *I can help them learn much more if they study here, at the oratory.*

"I need a corner of your kitchen," he announced to Mama Margaret.

Mama Margaret was pulling loaves of bread out of the oven. She looked over her shoulder. "What on earth are you going to do in the kitchen?"

"We are going to teach the boys here, at the oratory, instead of sending them into the city for school," Don Bosco said. "If they are here, we can teach them reading, writing, and arithmetic. But we can also teach them a trade—carpentry, or shoemaking, or metalworking. That way, when they grow up, they will have a skill and be able to find a job."

"And you want to turn my kitchen into a carpentry shop," Mama Margaret said.

"Well, I thought we would put the shoemaking shop in the kitchen," Don Bosco smiled. "But just in one corner!"

So Don Bosco and the boys set up a shoemaking station in the kitchen and a carpentry shop in the hallway. As the oratory grew, so did the trade schools. Don Bosco hired teachers to instruct the boys. He wanted to make sure they would be able to work when they left the oratory.

"Mama Margaret—that's Don Bosco's mother—cooks breakfast for us. We all help with the dishes," another chimed in.

Meanwhile, the seeds of Don Bosco's religious congregation were beginning to grow, too. On October 3, 1852, something very special happened. Michael Rua and Joseph Rocchietti (Roh-KYET-tee) became seminarians. Don Bosco continued to teach them and explain his vision for the future. Other young men joined them.

On January 26, 1854, four of the young men—Michael Rua, Joseph Rocchietti, James Artiglia (Ar-TEEL-ya), and John Cagliero—were with Don Bosco when he told them what name their group would have.

"We will be called 'Salesians,'" he said, "after Saint Francis de Sales."

The seminarians looked at one another. Don Bosco smiled.

"Do you want to know why?" he asked them. They nodded eagerly.

"Saint Francis de Sales will be our patron because we need to be clear teachers of the Faith to the young people we help. But this is how we will teach the Faith—with gentleness, kindness, and goodness just as Saint Francis de Sales did. We'll be ourselves and not overly serious all the time. We will draw young people to us through our goodness and joy. Then we will lead them to God."

The third important date for the new Salesian congregation was March 25, 1855. It was the feast of the Annunciation. In a small room at the oratory, Michael Rua knelt down. Don Bosco and several of the young men and seminarians were gathered around him. Michael made private vows of poverty, chastity, and obedience.

They were private vows because the Salesian congregation was not an official congregation yet. Any new religious order needs approval from the bishop and then from the pope. Don Bosco was not yet sure if the Salesians would ever be an official congregation in the Church.

That evening, Don Bosco paused before going to sleep. He was filled with gratitude.

Thank you, God, he prayed, *for the work that you have given me to do. Thank you for the young men you are sending to help me. Show me what to do next.*

15

A New Student

Boys were coming to the oratories for many different reasons. Some were like Bartholomew Garelli, the first boy Don Bosco had met all those years ago. They didn't remember their prayers, understand much about God, or know how to read or write. The oratory gave them an education. Others were like the boy who had come to the oratory on that rainy night, asking for a place to sleep. These boys were living on the streets or in places that were not safe. They needed a secure place to stay. The oratory provided that. Still other boys came because they wanted to study and work in a place where there was prayer, education, work, and good, wholesome fun. Some of them wanted to be priests.

In his travels around Italy, Don Bosco met families who wanted their sons to have a good religious education. He invited them to the oratory. Sometimes the families were able to pay a little money. This helped to support the oratory. But Don Bosco invited the boys whether or not their families could contribute financially.

"What about you?" Don Bosco asked one mother. "Would your son like to come to the oratory?"

"Oh, yes," the mother said. "We want our son to go to the oratory very much. But . . ."

"What is it?" Don Bosco asked kindly.

"We are very poor and we can't afford to pay you anything."

"That's all right," Don Bosco assured her. "Send your son to the oratory. God will provide. The most important thing is to give young people a chance to know God."

On October 2, 1854, Don Bosco was at home in Becchi for a few days with his brother Joseph. A man and his son came from a neighboring village to see him.

"I am Charles Savio (SAH-vee-oh)," the man said, "and this is my son Dominic."

"Ah, yes," Don Bosco said. "My friend Don Cugliero (Koo-lee-AIR-oh) told me about you. Dominic is his student, isn't he?"

"Yes, Father," Mr. Savio replied. "Dominic went to school in Castelnuovo before we moved. Now he studies there with Don Cugliero."

"And I want to be a priest," Dominic said.

"Why do you want to be a priest?" Don Bosco asked.

"I want to go to heaven and help other people go to heaven," Dominic replied.

Don Bosco smiled. "Would you like to come to the oratory in Turin and study there?" he asked.

"Oh, yes, Father!" Dominic exclaimed.

"Very good, very good," Don Bosco said. "You are good cloth."

Dominic and his father looked puzzled. "Good cloth?" Dominic asked. "Good cloth for what?"

"To make a beautiful garment for Our Lady," Don Bosco replied. "With our lives, each of us can become a beautiful garment for Our Lady, Help of Christians. And I see good cloth in you."

Indeed, Dominic Savio was very "good cloth." He went to the oratory in Turin at the end of October in 1854. On December 8, Dominic consecrated himself to Jesus through Mary. He did this by asking the Virgin Mary's special protection and prayers for his life. He also dedicated himself again to the goals he had set when he received his first Holy Communion.

I will go to confession and Holy Communion often, he reminded himself. *I will make*

Sundays special days for God. My friends will be Jesus and Mary. And I will choose death rather than sin.

Although Dominic was only twelve or thirteen, Don Bosco noticed that there was something special about how he lived his faith. One day after Mass, Dominic came to him.

"Don Bosco," he said, "today you said something very beautiful in your homily."

"Is that so?" Don Bosco replied. "What was it?"

"You said that God wants everyone to become saints," Dominic said, his eyes shining.

"That is true," Don Bosco said. "God wants every one of us to be saints and to be with him in heaven."

"Then—I want to be a saint!" Dominic exclaimed. "I want to do everything I can to be a saint."

"Do you know one of the best things you can do, Dominic?" Don Bosco asked. "Help others to be holy. Our holiness should bring others to God."

Dominic took these words very seriously. In 1856, with a group of other boys, he started the Company of Mary Immaculate. The purpose of this group was to honor Mary and to help its members become holy.

Sometimes Don Bosco had to remind Dominic not to be too serious!

"Don't forget to smile, Dominic," Don Bosco would say.

"I'm trying to be holy," Dominic replied. "I want to be a saint."

"Yes, but holy people are happy people," Don Bosco reminded him. "They pray, but they also work and play."

"Then I can be holy while I study, or play ball, or . . .?" Dominic asked.

"Of course!" Don Bosco said.

Dominic smiled.

Sometimes the boys got in trouble when they played. One day, two boys got into a fight. At first they were just yelling at each other. But they became angrier and angrier, and soon they picked up rocks to throw at each other. When Dominic saw this, he ran in between the two boys.

"Get out of the way!" one of them shouted. "We're not fighting with you!"

"Maybe not," Dominic replied. "But you will have to hit me with a rock before you can hit each other."

The boys realized what they were doing. They dropped their rocks and forgave each other.

In the summer of 1856, Dominic became sick.

"Dominic, I think you should go home for the summer," Don Bosco told him.

"But I wanted to stay here," Dominic said, coughing.

"No, it will be better if you go home and recover from your illness. If you are better, you can come back at the beginning of the school year. All right?"

"All right," Dominic said.

Dominic did recover over the summer, and he returned to the Oratory of St. Francis de Sales when the school year started. But that winter he became sick again. This time it was even worse. Dominic stayed at the oratory for as long as he could, but on March 1, 1857, Don Bosco sent him home.

"Good-bye, Don Bosco," Dominic whispered. He looked very weak.

"Good-bye, Dominic," Don Bosco said. "God bless you."

16

MAMA MARGARET

A little more than a week later, Don Bosco received a letter. After he read it, he placed it on his desk. He made the Sign of the Cross and gazed out the window.

Michael Rua walked into his office.

"Are your seminary classes done for the day, Michael?" Don Bosco asked.

"Yes, Don Bosco," Michael replied. He noticed the sad look on Don Bosco's face.

"What is it, Don Bosco?" he asked.

Don Bosco paused. "Dominic Savio has died," he said. "This letter is from his family. He died on March 9."

Michael crossed himself, too. "He was so young," he said. "Not even fifteen years old."

"Yes," Don Bosco replied. "Now he will pray for all our boys in the oratories. Michael, I think that the boys should know more about his story. He is a good example for them to follow. I think I will write a little biography of our Dominic Savio."

Two years later, Don Bosco's biography of Dominic Savio was published. It made

Dominic's simple story well known among the Salesians and throughout Italy.

❖❖❖

Mama Margaret had her hands full. Sixty-eight years old, she cooked three meals a day for Don Bosco and the thirty to forty boys who lived at the oratory. On Sundays she cooked for the hundreds of boys who came to the oratory for Mass, prayer, and games. She grew vegetables, washed clothes, and mended socks—often long into the night.

"You work so hard, Mama," Don Bosco said one night, as he helped her with the mending. He was happy he had learned how to sew all those years ago.

"Ah, John," Mama Margaret sighed. "I am old now. Sometimes I think I cannot do this anymore. But then . . ."

Don Bosco looked at his mother. He pointed to the crucifix. Mama Margaret nodded.

"Yes," she said softly. "Yes, I do it for God."

In November of 1856, Mama Margaret became very sick. Don Bosco called the doctor.

"She has double pneumonia," the doctor said. "And she is sixty-eight years old now. I do not know if she will recover."

"It's all right, John," Mama Margaret said when the doctor had left. "If God is calling me from this life, I am ready."

Don Bosco told his brother Joseph about their mother's illness. He asked his friend Don Borel to bring Holy Communion to her. All the boys in the Oratory of St. Francis de Sales joined in praying for Mama Margaret.

On November 25, with her sons Joseph and John at her side, Mama Margaret died. Both men cried; then they prayed.

Don Bosco remembered what his mother had said to him when he became a priest. *You will pray for me too, won't you?* He stood up.

"I am going to say Mass for Mama's soul," he told Joseph. Joseph nodded. Don Bosco left to offer Mass.

After Mass, as he was walking back to the oratory, he thought about his mother. *She was like a mother to all our oratories,* he thought. *And she will still be a mother to us now.*

In that moment Don Bosco realized that his religious family had another Mother in heaven, as well.

Mary, Help of Christians, he prayed, *the Salesians still need a mother. The oratories need a mother. Now you must be our mother. Watch over us now and always.*

❖❖❖

Until then, the seminarians who were working with Don Bosco, like Michael Rua, had only been able to make private vows. Since the beginning, Don Bosco had prayed about the future of the group he had founded and dedicated to God under the protection of Saint Francis de Sales. Over the years, he gathered young men from the oratories and invited them to consider becoming priests committed to helping him in his work with young people.

In 1858, Don Bosco went to Rome to speak to Pope Pius IX. He showed him the rule of life he had written about how the Salesians would live. Pius IX encouraged him to go ahead with the foundation of the Salesian congregation.

On December 9, 1859, Don Bosco gathered all the seminarians and young men who were helping him. He cleared his throat.

"My friends," he said, "I asked you to come here tonight so that I could share something with you. For a long time now I have been thinking about founding a religious congregation. I think that now the time is right. Pope Pius IX has given us his blessing. It is time for the Salesians to begin a real religious congregation."

"But, Don Bosco," one young man spoke up, "I thought we were already a group of Salesians."

"A group, yes," Don Bosco replied. "And I know that some of you have made private vows. But now I believe that God wants us to officially begin the Salesians as a foundation in the Church."

Nobody was sure what to think. None of them knew how or if this would change what they had already been doing.

Leaning forward in his chair, Don Bosco continued. "So I am asking you: do you desire to belong to God through the vows of chastity, poverty, and obedience? Do you desire to dedicate yourself to serving him and serving young people as a Salesian? If so, then come back here in a week."

The young men fixed their eyes on Don Bosco. The room filled with silence; no one said anything.

"But it may be that God is not calling you to be a Salesian," Don Bosco said calmly. "If you feel that way, you may certainly remain at the oratory, and you will not be required to come back here next week."

Don Bosco stood up and left the room. All the young men looked around at one another. Each one of them had some praying to do—and a big decision to make.

17

THE FIRST SALESIANS

A week later, all but two of the men came back. Don Bosco took out a piece of paper.

"I have written about the Salesians here," he said. "Now I will read it to you.

"We will serve God by serving young people—especially young people who are at risk or in any kind of danger," Don Bosco read.

"We will live and work in the love of Jesus. The purpose of our congregation is to help us become holy, bring glory to God, and lead souls to Christ, especially those who need the most help."

He placed the paper and a pen on the table. First Don Bosco signed his name. Then, one by one, each of the men signed it, too. This was the first official act of the Salesian congregation.

After this, the Salesians began to grow quickly. Many more steps would need to take place before the congregation could be officially recognized by the Church. But the first step had been taken. Don Bosco knew that God would bless them.

Some men wanted to help Don Bosco, but they did not feel that God was calling them to become priests or to make religious vows of poverty, chastity, and obedience. There were women who wanted to help, too. A group of them came to see Don Bosco.

"We think you are doing wonderful work, Don Bosco," one of them said. "You are helping so many young boys to know God, to study, and to find good work."

"Yes, God is blessing our work," said Don Bosco.

"But how can we help you with this work?" the woman asked. "We don't have any money to give you, but we are good cooks. Perhaps there is cooking or laundry that we could do."

"That would be wonderful!" exclaimed Don Bosco. "Your help would be most welcome. Since my mother died, we have not had many women at the oratory. If you come, you will help the boys learn how to treat women with respect."

Other people donated money or food to the oratory. Don Bosco called all these people "Salesian Cooperators."

❖❖❖

In 1860, Michael Rua was ordained to the priesthood. Then in 1862, the twenty-two first Salesians made their first public vows. This means that they promised, in a ceremony in church, to give up the chance to be married and have children, to live with few possessions, and to do whatever Church and religious authorities asked of them. As Salesians, they also dedicated themselves to taking care of young people.

This was a very happy time for Don Bosco. But in 1862, he had another dream. This one was very troubling.

"Imagine that you are with me on the shore of a great sea," he shared with the first Salesians. "There are countless ships, all ready for battle. They are attacking another ship that is much bigger and higher than theirs. The captain of the big ship is the pope.

"In the distance, there are two pillars. On top of one pillar, there is a statue of Mary, Help of Christians. On top of the other, there is a Host.

"There are also some smaller ships defending the big ship. The captains of these ships board the big ship. They have a meeting about what to do, but they are interrupted by a storm. Then they have a second meeting, but an even bigger storm comes. The pope steers the ship toward the two pillars.

"The enemy ships continue to attack the big ship. The pope is wounded by gunfire. The first time he gets up. But he is wounded again, and this time he dies. But another pope takes his place and continues to steer the ship toward the two pillars.

"Rain, lightning, waves, and gunfire batter the big ship, but it continues on its way. When it reaches the two pillars, the pope anchors the ship to the pillars—on one side, to the pillar with Mary; on the other side, to the pillar with the Host.

"The enemy ships disappear! And the smaller ships that defended the big ship come to anchor themselves to the pillars, too."

There was silence when Don Bosco finished telling them his dream.

"What does it mean?" Don Rua asked.

"I'm not sure," Don Bosco sighed. "It may mean that the Church will be persecuted in the future. But whatever it means, one thing is sure. We must stay close to Mary, Help of Christians, and to the Eucharist. Never forget that."

Later that year, Don Bosco startled the other Salesians.

"We need to build a church," he said.

"What?" they asked in surprise.

"The chapel at the Oratory of Saint Francis de Sales is too small. Besides, the Salesian Society is growing, and we need to thank Mary, Help of Christians. She protects and helps us. All the graces that God gives us come through her. She is the patron of the Salesian Society, and we are going to build a big church in her honor."

"But where?" they asked.

Don Bosco pointed to an open area across from the chapel.

"How will we ever get the money?" his companions asked.

Don Bosco smiled. "The Blessed Mother wants the church," he said. "She will take care of the money."

The next year, in May of 1863, construction began on the church. There were many obstacles! Often construction had to stop because the money ran out. One time the contractor came to Don Bosco to demand the money.

"You can take all the money I have," Don Bosco said. He opened his wallet and shook four pennies into the contractor's hands. Then he laughed.

"Well, Mary, Help of Christians will have to do better than that!"

And she did. Every time work stopped because the money ran out, someone came with a donation so that work could begin again. The walls of the church grew higher and higher.

Mary, Help of Christians, this will be your church, Don Bosco prayed. *This is the Salesian Society's gift to you. Thank you for taking care of us.*

❖❖❖

Around this time, Don Bosco had another very special dream.

He was crossing the town square in Turin. The square was full of screaming, noisy girls. They were running around and chasing one another. A few girls stood apart from the rest. These girls came over to Don Bosco.

"We have been neglected," they said to him.

Don Bosco didn't know what they meant. Then a beautiful lady appeared in the midst of the girls. The lady looked at Don Bosco.

"Take care of these girls," she said. "They are my children."

Don Bosco had this dream twice and found himself thinking about it a lot. It was very similar to the dreams he'd had about the boys in the field when he was a boy himself. *Mary, Help of Christians, are you asking me to take care of girls, too? But how can I do that?* He wondered.

18
Grigio

There were some people who were suspicious of Don Bosco and did not like the work that he and the Salesians were doing. Some of them thought that Don Bosco was gathering boys at the oratory for a political purpose, and that he planned to start a revolution. Other people were angry because the boys who used to work long hours in their factories were now going to school at the oratory. Some of the boys still worked at the factories, but not as many and not as long as they previously had. These people were angry with Don Bosco for taking their workers away.

At times, people were so upset that they tried to attack Don Bosco or threatened to do him harm. They knew that in the evenings he often visited someone who was sick or dying. Usually it was quite late—even the middle of the night—when he would walk back to the oratory alone. He had been attacked before. But God soon sent protection for him.

One night, Don Bosco was walking back from visiting a sick man. He was walking through an area where he had been attacked before. He started praying that he would be safe. Then he saw a large gray dog. At first he was afraid. *What if the dog attacks me?* he thought.

But the dog came right up to Don Bosco and rubbed his head against Don Bosco's leg. Don Bosco reached down to pet the dog, and the dog wagged his tail happily.

"Well, my friend," Don Bosco said, "have you been sent to protect me? Let's go, then."

The dog walked with Don Bosco all the way back to the oratory. Then he disappeared. This happened over and over again. Don Bosco began calling the dog "Grigio" (GREE-joe), which means "gray one" in Italian, because of the dog's gray color.

Grigio protected Don Bosco from danger many times. One night Don Bosco needed to go to another part of the city of Turin. As he left, he saw Grigio lying at the gate of the oratory.

"Ah, there you are!" Don Bosco said. "Come on, Grigio, let's go."

But Grigio growled and would not let Don Bosco walk past. No matter what Don Bosco tried, Grigio would not let him leave

"Well, my friend," Don Bosco said, "have you been sent to protect me? Let's go, then."

the oratory. Don Bosco didn't know what to do, so he went back inside the oratory.

A few minutes later, a man knocked at the door.

"Don't let Don Bosco go out tonight," he said to the boy who answered the door. "There are some men waiting for him on the road. They disagree with what he is doing at the oratory, and they are planning to attack him!"

❖❖❖

Don Bosco was a busy man! Every morning he prayed and wrote. He heard confessions before celebrating Mass. Sometimes as many as fifty boys were waiting to go to confession!

After Mass he always made time to play games with the boys for a few minutes before they went to school and he went to work. There were always people to see and letters to write. Sometimes, even miracles took place in his office.

One day a woman and her nine-year-old son were waiting to see Don Bosco. The boy's legs were crippled. He had never walked in his life.

"How are you, my friend?" Don Bosco smiled at the boy.

"Please help my son, Don Bosco," the mother pleaded.

"God will help your son," Don Bosco replied. "Trust in Mary, Help of Christians—trust her completely." Then he blessed the boy and told him, "Mary, Help of Christians will take care of you. Now, take a step toward me."

The boy stood up. He took one step, then another. He was walking! His mother gasped. God had healed her son through the prayers of Don Bosco and the Blessed Mother!

Because of stories like this, Don Bosco was becoming quite famous in Italy. Many priests wanted him to come and preach at their parishes.

"I am going to the parish in Montemagno (Mon-tay-MAG-no) this week," he said to Don Rua one morning in 1864.

"Are you preaching there, Don Bosco?" Don Rua asked.

"Yes," Don Bosco replied. "I am preaching for three nights to prepare the people for the feast of Mary's Assumption."

"I have heard that there is a terrible drought in Montemagno," Don Rua said. "They have not had any rain there for a long time. It's destroying the crops there."

"Is that so?" Don Bosco said. "We will have to pray for rain then."

The first night Don Bosco gave a wonderful homily. He wanted to help the people trust in God. At the end of his homily he said, "God will always take care of you. The Blessed Mother will always take care of you. But you must trust in God. Go to confession, receive Holy Communion, and pray to Mary, Help of Christians. God will hear your prayers for rain."

After the homily, the pastor of the parish came to Don Bosco.

"What do you think you're doing?" he asked abruptly.

"What do you mean?" Don Bosco replied.

"You promised the people that it will rain if they receive the sacraments and pray! How can you make such a promise? And what will we do when it doesn't rain?"

"Don't worry, Father," Don Bosco answered. "Just pray and trust more, not less."

The next two nights the church was full of people coming to listen to Don Bosco. They went to confession. They received Holy Communion. They prayed the Rosary, and asked the Blessed Mother to help them.

"Will it really rain when you finish preaching, Don Bosco?" they asked.

"Pray and trust," was all Don Bosco would say.

The feast of the Assumption, the last day that Don Bosco was going to preach, was hot and sunny. In the evening, there was only one small cloud in the clear sky.

Dear Blessed Mother, Don Bosco prayed, *please send rain to these poor people. You see how much they have prayed and trusted. Now it is my turn. I trust that you will not fail them.*

A few minutes later, Don Bosco stood up to preach. He prayed a "Hail Mary" with the people. Then he began his homily. But no one could hear him because, at that very moment, thunder boomed, lightning flashed, and rain began to pour down!

Don Bosco smiled. *Thank you, Blessed Mother!*

Then he led the people in prayers of thanksgiving.

❖❖❖

God blessed Don Bosco's preaching and the meetings he had with people in his office with miracles. But miracles occurred in other places, too. Sometimes they were miracles of healing, like the little boy with the crippled legs. Sometimes, through Don Bosco's prayers, God led a person back to the

Church and the sacraments. And sometimes God worked a miracle to help Don Bosco when he or the oratory was in need.

One morning Don Bosco was hearing confessions. In between confessions, one of the boys came to him and said, "Don Bosco, there is no bread for breakfast."

"That's impossible," Don Bosco said. "Go look again."

A few minutes later, the boy returned.

"Don Bosco, we have looked everywhere. All we can find are a few rolls."

"Hmm," said Don Bosco. "Then go to the baker and ask him for what we need."

"We can't do that!" the boy exclaimed. "We owe the baker a lot of money, and he will not let us have any more bread."

"Well, then God will have to send what we need. Put the rolls in a basket and I will come and hand them out."

Don Bosco left the confessional and went to the dining room. He took the basket of bread and counted the rolls—fifteen. He looked at the boys—three hundred. He closed his eyes, prayed silently, and then motioned to the boys to come and get their bread.

For the next several minutes, Don Bosco handed out the bread. Boy after boy came up; boy after boy received a roll. After the last boy had taken a roll, Don Bosco looked down into the basket. There were fifteen rolls left. God had truly sent all the bread they needed!

19

DAUGHTERS OF MARY, HELP OF CHRISTIANS

In the city of Mornese (More-NAY-zay), southeast of Turin, there was a group of young women called the Daughters of Mary Immaculate. These women gathered every week for prayer. They served the parish and the people of the area.

One of these women was named Mary Mazzarello (Mah-tsah-RELL-oh). Mary was born in 1837. She was a kind girl and a hard worker. She wanted to be very close to God. When she was eighteen years old, she joined the Daughters of Mary Immaculate.

With the other Daughters of Mary Immaculate, Mary performed all kinds of good works. She taught mothers and girls how to sew and how to understand more about their Catholic faith. She nursed the sick when an epidemic of typhoid fever broke out. With another woman, she opened a dressmaking shop and took in orphans.

In 1864, Don Bosco visited Mornese and met with the Daughters of Mary Immaculate.

He thought the work they were doing was wonderful. He noticed how holy and prayerful they were. But he noticed something special about Mary. He saw her great desire to love God, and he saw how kind she was with the children she took care of. When he met Mary, Don Bosco remembered his dream about the girls.

Maybe God wants me to begin a congregation of sisters, too, he thought. *And perhaps this woman is the one he has chosen to help me.*

Don Bosco didn't know it, but Mary had also had a dream. In it she was walking in the hills outside Mornese. She saw a large building with open courtyards. Many girls were playing in the courtyards. She heard a voice say, "I entrust these girls to you."

So when Don Bosco asked her if she was willing to help him, Mary quickly agreed.

Just like with the Salesian Society, it took a long time to officially begin the congregation of sisters. Don Bosco and Mary Mazzarello named the congregation the Daughters of Mary, Help of Christians.

"Our Lady, Help of Christians will be the foundress of this congregation," Don Bosco told the sisters. "She will help and protect everything you do."

The Salesian Society and the Daughters of Mary, Help of Christians quickly spread all over Italy. *Now what are you asking, Lord? What do you want next?* Don Bosco prayed.

One morning Don Bosco came to breakfast with a big smile on his face.

"I've had the most exciting dream!" he announced. "In my dream, I saw a land that I did not recognize, a land that I had never seen before. I was on a huge plain, and in the distance there were mountains. All over the plain there were men with long hair and dark skin. I don't know what country they belonged to.

"Some of the men were running, some were hunting, and some were fighting with one another. As I watched, I saw a group of missionaries. They had come to preach the Gospel. But the native men did not give them a chance—they beat the missionaries and killed them.

"Then another group of missionaries came. They were young. They looked like Salesians, and I even recognized some of them. I tried to stop them, because I thought the native men would kill them, too.

"But they didn't! When the native men saw the Salesians, they put down their weapons and listened to them. The missionaries taught them about God. They taught them prayers, hymns, and the Rosary. I heard them praying and singing, and then—

"I woke up," finished Don Bosco. "But do you see? Now I know that the Salesians must go beyond Italy. They must be missionaries to lands where people do not know about God. They must bring the joy of God to all people!"

The Salesian Society had already been invited to go to France. Don Bosco was happy to send his Salesians there. But he kept thinking about his dream. He read about many different countries to see if he could recognize the land and people from his dream. He read about Ethiopia, China, Australia, and many others.

Then one day in December of 1874, a messenger from the archbishop of Buenos Aires (BWAY-nos AIY-rays), Argentina, came to talk to Don Bosco.

"The archbishop wants the Salesians to come to Buenos Aires," the messenger said. He described the land and people of Argentina to Don Bosco. Don Bosco's eyes began to shine.

"This is it!" he exclaimed. "Argentina is the land from my dream! The Salesians will go to Buenos Aires."

In 1875, ten Salesians traveled to Buenos Aires. Before they left, Don Bosco wrote some advice for them.

"Think only of souls.

"Be especially tender with the sick, children, the elderly, and the poor.

"Always be respectful and obedient to the authorities.

"Do what you can, and leave the rest to God. Trust in Jesus and in Mary, Help of Christians."

This was only the beginning of the Salesians' missionary activity. In 1881, they went to Spain, and in 1887, to England. After that came Portugal and other European countries.

Many Salesians also went to South America. In all, he sent eleven groups of Salesian missionaries to South America: to Uruguay, Brazil, Chile, and Ecuador.

Don Bosco always took special care to send these missionaries off with many prayers and his blessing.

Meanwhile, the Daughters of Mary, Help of Christians were spreading, too. In 1876, thirty-six sisters left the first house in Mornese to open seven houses in different regions of Italy. In 1877, they followed the

Salesian Society to Uruguay, Argentina, Chile, and France.

"It makes me very happy," Don Bosco said, "to see Salesians all over the world."

20
"Love One Another"

"How are you, Mother Mazzarello?" Don Bosco asked. He had heard that Mary Mazzarello's health was declining, and he had come to visit her. It was February of 1881.

"I am tired," Mother Mazzarello said to Don Bosco. "I have just returned from France. The sisters are opening a new house in Marseilles (Mar-SAY)."

"That is wonderful," Don Bosco said. "But you need to take some time to rest."

"I will," Mother Mazzarello replied. "But you know, Don Bosco, I always remember our Salesian motto."

Don Bosco smiled.

"'Give me souls,'" Mother Mazzarello said prayerfully. "'Give me souls, and take away the rest.'"

"Yes," Don Bosco said, "for the mission of all the Salesians is to love people's souls and bring them to God, especially the youngest, poorest, and neediest souls."

"This mission is so beautiful," Mother Mazzarello said. "I would willingly offer my life for it."

Just a few months later, on May 14, 1881, Mary Mazzarello died. She was forty-four years old at the time of her death. Though her life had been short, it had also been fruitful. The work she left behind was carried on by 139 sisters, fifty novices (young women preparing to be sisters), and twenty-six religious houses.

❖❖❖

Pope Leo XIII had heard about Don Bosco's work with young people and his success in building the Church of Mary, Help of Christians. In the last years of his life, the pope had a special mission for him.

"The Vatican does not yet have a church dedicated to the Sacred Heart," the pope told Don Bosco. "We bought the land to build the church on. We even began building, but we had to stop because we ran out of money. I would like you to supervise the project."

"I always want to say yes to you, Holy Father," Don Bosco said, "but I am sixty-five years old now. Let me go back to Turin and ask the advice of my brother Salesians."

Don Rua and the other Salesians were worried that taking on this project would be too much for Don Bosco. But Don Bosco reminded them that it was important to be generous in service. They decided to say yes to the Holy Father's request, and so Don Bosco returned to Rome.

There were many obstacles in building this church, just as there had been with the Church of Mary, Help of Christians. In fact, it took seven years to finish the church! But finally, on May 14, 1887, the Church of the Sacred Heart in Rome was consecrated.

Don Bosco was happy return to Turin when the task was done. He liked walking through the oratory and seeing the boys studying, working, praying, and playing. He especially loved to pray in the Church of Mary, Help of Christians. And now he had time to reflect on his life.

Don Bosco's days were full of memories and gratitude. He remembered when he was just a boy, walking on tightropes and performing juggling acts to help people learn about God. He remembered attending school and then seminary with Luigi, his best friend who had died before ordination. He recalled meeting the very first boy he helped, Bartholomew Garelli, in the sacristy of the Church of St. Francis of Assisi. And he remembered the faces of the hundreds and thousands of boys he had welcomed to the oratory since then. He thought about all the difficulties and trials, as well as all the joys and happiness he had experienced serving God and trusting in him to provide. He could never have imagined that his life would have turned out as it had.

But especially, Don Bosco thought about his dreams, and how the Blessed Mother had entrusted young boys—and then girls—to his care.

Now the Salesian Society and the Daughters of Mary, Help of Christians are doing what the Blessed Mother told me to do, he thought. *They are helping people to know God. They are showing young boys and girls how much God loves them. They are bringing joy all over the world!*

In November of 1887, Don Bosco began to feel the length of his years more and more. By the end of the month, he was tired and sick. He could no longer work. In early December, he celebrated Mass for the last time.

News spread quickly that Don Bosco was ill with a very serious infection. Many Salesian priests and brothers came to visit him. Many important people in Italy came to see him, too. Even people from other countries came! Don Bosco listened to them, gave them advice, and heard their confessions.

Bishop Cagliero, one of the first Salesian missionaries, came from Argentina to see Don Bosco. He had heard a mysterious voice in prayer saying, "Go to Turin to be with Don Bosco at his death."

In all the Salesian houses around the world, the boys and girls prayed daily for Don Bosco. He was like a father to them, even to the ones he had never met.

Don Bosco was too weak to walk. During his last month, the Salesians had to carry him when he needed to go from one place to another.

"Put this on my bill," he joked with them.

Even though he was no longer able to work, Don Bosco's heart was centered on his mission to reach young people and help them to know God. He told Bishop Cagliero, "Save many souls in your missions." And when the Superior General of the Daughters of Mary, Help of Christians came to see him, he told her, "Tell the sisters to do all they can to save many souls."

But Don Bosco also expressed concern for those who had been called to share the work God and the Blessed Mother had begun through him. He gave his last advice to the Salesian Society through Don Rua and Bishop Cagliero.

"You must treat one another as brothers," he whispered. "Love one another. Mary, Help of Christians, will always help you."

On January 28, 1888, he said, "Tell the boys I am waiting for them in heaven." He died three days later, on January 31, 1888, surrounded by his Salesian brothers. He was seventy-two years old.

❖❖❖

Don Bosco was beatified by Pope Pius XI on March 19, 1929. He was canonized by the same pope on Easter Sunday, April 1, 1934. His feast day is January 31. Saint John Bosco is the patron saint of young people, apprentices learning a trade, stage magicians, and of Catholic publishers and editors.

Mary Mazzarello was canonized by Pope Pius XII on June 24, 1951.

Nearly a hundred years after his death, Dominic Savio was declared a saint by Pope Pius XII, on June 12, 1954.

Mama Margaret was declared venerable (the first step to being declared a saint) on October 23, 2006 by Pope Benedict XVI.

At the time of Don Bosco's death, there were about 750 Salesian priests and brothers, 250 novices, and 65 religious houses.

After Don Bosco's death, the Salesian Society began to be called the "Salesians of Don Bosco." Throughout the world today, there are approximately 17,000 Salesians of Don Bosco, 15,000 Daughters of Mary, Help of Christians, and 27,000 Salesian Cooperators. They have houses in more than 130 countries, and are the third largest family of religious orders in the Church today.

Still today, the Salesians of Don Bosco and the Daughters of Mary, Help of Christians carry on the work of Saint John Bosco. They live by his words, and they invite young people to live by these same words:

"Let us serve the Lord with holy cheerfulness. Let us love."

Prayer

Saint John Bosco, you loved Jesus very much. You wanted to tell other people, especially young people, how much Jesus loves them. You were creative in doing this! Whether you were juggling or teaching class, playing games or hearing confessions, you were always loving.

Help me to love Jesus, too. Help me to see the opportunities that I have to tell others about his love. Some of these opportunities might be in school or at home. Others might be when I'm playing or talking with my friends. In everything I do, help me to be loving like you were.

You taught boys and girls to love Jesus with a smile. Help me to love Jesus with a smile, too. You are a special patron of young people. When you died, you said you would wait for us in heaven. Please pray for me now, so that one day I may meet you in heaven. Pray for me, so that during my life, I can love Jesus and love others. Amen.

Glossary

1. **Anointing of the Sick**—the sacrament in which the Holy Spirit strengthens and gives courage and peace to someone who is seriously ill. God's Spirit, through this sacrament, forgives sin and heals the soul. God sometimes uses this sacrament as a means of physical healing as well.

2. **Beatification**—the ceremony in which the Church recognizes that a baptized Catholic, who has died, lived a life of Gospel holiness in a heroic way. In most cases, a proven miracle obtained through the holy person's prayers to God is also required. A person who is beatified is given the title "Blessed".

3. **Canonization**—the ceremony in which the pope officially declares that someone is a saint in heaven. To canonize someone is to recognize that he or she has lived a life of heroic virtue, is worthy of imitation, and can intercede for others. Canonization comes after beatification. Like beatification, canonization requires a miracle resulting from the holy person's prayers to God.

4. **Catechism**—instruction on the truths of our Catholic faith and explanations of Church teaching so that we may live by them, learn about God, and grow closer to him.

5. **Cathedral**—the main church in a diocese where a bishop serves.

6. **Chaplain**—a priest who cares for the spiritual needs of a particular group of people, such as those in a hospital.

7. **Consecrate**—to set aside a person or an object for God or God's service.

8. **Constitutions**—the rule of life, or organized method of living, of a particular religious community.

9. **Devotions**—special prayers or practices performed to honor God, Mary, or a saint.

10. **Diocese**—a part of the Church made up of Catholics within a certain geographical area.

11. **Don**—Italian for "Father" (as a priest).

12. **Franciscan**—a person who vows to follow the Rule of Saint Francis of Assisi as members of a religious order founded by Saint Francis or associated with how he

lived the vows of poverty, chastity, and obedience.

13. **Grace**—the gift of God's life alive in the human soul. Sanctifying grace is the lasting presence of God in us that makes us holy, more like him. We receive sanctifying grace at Baptism. Actual grace is the assistance God offers us during our life to help us perform good actions.

14. **Mission**—a special work performed for God to help others experience God's love and inspire them to love him in return.

15. **Oratory**—(as used by Saint John Bosco) a Salesian house where young people are taken care of, educated, trained in a trade, and instructed in the Catholic faith.

16. **Ordination**—the ceremony during which a man receives the sacrament of Holy Orders. A man may be ordained a deacon, a priest, or a bishop.

17. **Religious congregation**—a group of men or women who have taken religious vows and usually live together in one or more communities; an official religious order, often founded by a saint, within the Church.

18. **Sacristy**—a room near the sanctuary of a church used for storing the things needed for the celebration of Mass. Priests usually put on and take off their vestments in the sacristy.

19. **Seminary**—a place where men study and prepare to become priests.

20. **Venerable**—a title given to a person who is being considered for canonization but has not yet been beatified. A person with the title "Venerable" has lived a life of heroic virtue.

21. **Vow**—an important promise freely made to God.

Pauline BOOKS & MEDIA

The Daughters of St. Paul operate book and media centers at the following addresses. Visit, call, or write the one nearest you today, or find us at www.paulinestore.org.

CALIFORNIA
3908 Sepulveda Blvd, Culver City, CA 90230 — 310-397-8676
3250 Middlefield Road, Menlo Park, CA 94025 — 650-369-4230

FLORIDA
145 S.W. 107th Avenue, Miami, FL 33174 — 305-559-6715

HAWAII
1143 Bishop Street, Honolulu, HI 96813 — 808-521-2731

ILLINOIS
172 North Michigan Avenue, Chicago, IL 60601 — 312-346-4228

LOUISIANA
4403 Veterans Memorial Blvd, Metairie, LA 70006 — 504-887-7631

MASSACHUSETTS
885 Providence Hwy, Dedham, MA 02026 — 781-326-5385

MISSOURI
9804 Watson Road, St. Louis, MO 63126 — 314-965-3512

NEW YORK
115 E. 29th Street, New York City, NY 10016 — 212-754-1110

SOUTH CAROLINA
243 King Street, Charleston, SC 29401 — 843-577-0175

TEXAS
No book center; for parish exhibits or outreach evangelization, contact: 210-569-0500, or SanAntonio@paulinemedia.com, or P.O. Box 761416, San Antonio, TX 78245

VIRGINIA
1025 King Street, Alexandria, VA 22314 — 703-549-3806

CANADA
3022 Dufferin Street, Toronto, ON M6B 3T5 — 416-781-9131